THIS BOOK
BELONGS TO

Books by Roald Dahl

THE BFG
BOY: TALES OF CHILDHOOD
CHARLIE AND THE CHOCOLATE FACTORY
CHARLIE AND THE GREAT GLASS ELEVATOR
THE COMPLETE ADVENTURES OF CHARLIE AND MR WILLY WONKA
DANNY THE CHAMPION OF THE WORLD
GEORGE'S MARVELLOUS MEDICINE
GOING SOLO
JAMES AND THE GIANT PEACH
MATILDA
THE WITCHES

For younger readers

THE ENORMOUS CROCODILE
ESIO TROT
FANTASTIC MR FOX
THE GIRAFFE AND THE PELLY AND ME
THE MAGIC FINGER
THE TWITS

Picture books

DIRTY BEASTS (*with Quentin Blake*)
THE ENORMOUS CROCODILE (*with Quentin Blake*)
THE GIRAFFE AND THE PELLY AND ME (*with Quentin Blake*)
THE MINPINS (*with Patrick Benson*)
REVOLTING RHYMES (*with Quentin Blake*)

Plays

THE BFG: PLAYS FOR CHILDREN (*Adapted by David Wood*)
CHARLIE AND THE CHOCOLATE FACTORY: A PLAY (*Adapted by Richard George*)
DANNY THE CHAMPION OF THE WORLD: PLAYS FOR CHILDREN (*Adapted by David Wood*)
FANTASTIC MR FOX: A PLAY (*Adapted by Sally Reid*)
JAMES AND THE GIANT PEACH: A PLAY (*Adapted by Richard George*)
THE TWITS: PLAYS FOR CHILDREN (*Adapted by David Wood*)
THE WITCHES: PLAYS FOR CHILDREN (*Adapted by David Wood*)

Teenage fiction

THE GREAT AUTOMATIC GRAMMATIZATOR AND OTHER STORIES
RHYME STEW
SKIN AND OTHER STORIES
THE VICAR OF NIBBLESWICKE
THE WONDERFUL STORY OF HENRY SUGAR AND SIX MORE

Collections

THE ROALD DAHL TREASURY
SONGS AND VERSE

Roald Dahl

Fantastic Mr Fox

The Enormous Crocodile

The Giraffe and the Pelly and Me

illustrated by Quentin Blake

PUFFIN

Find out more about Roald Dahl by visiting the website at
roalddahl.com

PUFFIN BOOKS

Published by the Penguin Group
Penguin Books Ltd, 80 Strand, London WC2R 0RL, England
Penguin Group (USA) Inc., 375 Hudson Street, New York, New York 10014, USA
Penguin Group (Canada), 90 Eglinton Avenue East, Suite 700, Toronto, Ontario, Canada M4P 2Y3
(a division of Pearson Penguin Canada Inc.)
Penguin Ireland, 25 St Stephen's Green, Dublin 2, Ireland (a division of Penguin Books Ltd)
Penguin Group (Australia), 250 Camberwell Road, Camberwell, Victoria 3124, Australia
(a division of Pearson Australia Group Pty Ltd)
Penguin Books India Pvt Ltd, 11 Community Centre, Panchsheel Park, New Delhi – 110 017, India
Penguin Group (NZ), 67 Apollo Drive, Rosedale, Auckland 0632, New Zealand
(a division of Pearson New Zealand Ltd)
Penguin Books (South Africa) (Pty) Ltd, Block D, Rosebank Office Park, 181 Jan Smuts Avenue, Parktown North, Gauteng 2193, South Africa

Penguin Books Ltd, Registered Offices: 80 Strand, London WC2R 0RL, England

puffinbooks.com

This collection published 2012
001 – 10 9 8 7 6 5 4 3 2 1

Fantastic Mr Fox first published by George Allen and Unwin 1970
Published in Puffin Books 1974
Published with illustrations by Quentin Blake 1996
Colour edition published 1998

Colour treatment by Vida Williams

The Enormous Crocodile first published by Jonathan Cape 1978
Published in Puffin Books 1980

The Giraffe and the Pelly and Me first published in Great Britain by Jonathan Cape and in the USA by Farrar, Straus and Giroux, 1985
Published in Puffin Books 1987

Made and printed in China

British Library Cataloguing in Publication Data
A CIP catalogue record for this book is available from the British Library

ISBN: 978–0–141–34623–6

CONTENTS

Fantastic Mr Fox 1

The Enormous Crocodile 83

The Giraffe and the Pelly and Me 117

Fantastic Mr Fox

~ To Olivia ~

CONTENTS

1	The Three Farmers	1
2	Mr Fox	7
3	The Shooting	10
4	The Terrible Shovels	15
5	The Terrible Tractors	20
6	The Race	24
7	'We'll Never Let Him Go'	29
8	The Foxes Begin to Starve	31
9	Mr Fox Has a Plan	34
10	Boggis's Chicken House Number One	37
11	A Surprise for Mrs Fox	43
12	Badger	45
13	Bunce's Giant Storehouse	50
14	Badger Has Doubts	58
15	Bean's Secret Cider Cellar	61
16	The Woman	67
17	The Great Feast	72
18	Still Waiting	80

Chapter One

THE THREE FARMERS

Down in the valley there were three farms. The owners of these farms had done well. They were rich men. They were also nasty men. All three of them were about as nasty and mean as any men you could meet. Their names were Farmer Boggis, Farmer Bunce and Farmer Bean.

Boggis was a chicken farmer. He kept thousands of chickens. He was enormously fat. This was because he ate three boiled chickens smothered with dumplings every day for breakfast, lunch and supper.

Bunce was a duck-and-goose farmer. He kept thousands of ducks and geese. He was a kind of pot-bellied dwarf. He was so short his chin would have been underwater in the shallow end of any swimming-pool in the world. His food was doughnuts and goose-livers. He mashed the livers into a disgusting paste and then stuffed the paste into the doughnuts. This diet gave him a tummy-ache and a beastly temper.

Bean was a turkey-and-apple farmer. He kept thousands of turkeys in an orchard full of apple trees. He never ate any food at all. Instead, he drank gallons of strong cider which he made from the apples in his orchard. He was as thin as a pencil and the cleverest of them all.

Boggis and Bunce and Bean
One fat, one short, one lean.
These horrible crooks
So different in looks
Were none the less equally mean.

That is what the children round about used to sing when they saw them.

Chapter Two

Mr Fox

On a hill above the valley there was a wood.

In the wood there was a huge tree.

Under the tree there was a hole.

In the hole lived Mr Fox and Mrs Fox and their four Small Foxes.

Every evening as soon as it got dark, Mr Fox would say to Mrs Fox, 'Well, my darling, what shall it be this time? A plump chicken from Boggis? A duck or a goose from Bunce? Or a nice turkey from Bean?' And when Mrs Fox had told him what she wanted, Mr Fox would creep down into the valley in the darkness of the night and help himself.

Boggis and Bunce and Bean knew very well what was going on, and it made them wild with rage. They were not men who liked to give anything away. Less still did they like anything to be stolen from them. So every night each of them would take his shotgun and hide in a dark place somewhere on his own farm, hoping to catch the robber.

But Mr Fox was too clever for them. He always approached a farm with the wind blowing in his face, and this meant that if any man were lurking in the shadows ahead, the wind would carry the smell of that man to Mr Fox's nose from far away. Thus, if Mr Boggis was hiding behind his Chicken House Number One, Mr Fox would smell him out from fifty yards off and quickly change direction, heading for Chicken House Number Four at the other end of the farm.

'Dang and blast that lousy beast!' cried Boggis.

'I'd like to rip his guts out!' said Bunce.

'He must be killed!' cried Bean.

'But how?' said Boggis. 'How on earth can we catch the blighter?'

Bean picked his nose delicately with a long finger. 'I have a plan,' he said.

'You've never had a decent plan yet,' said Bunce.

'Shut up and listen,' said Bean. 'Tomorrow night we will all hide just outside the hole where the fox lives. We will wait there until he comes out. Then . . . *Bang! Bang-bang-bang.*'

'Very clever,' said Bunce. 'But first we shall have to find the hole.'

'My dear Bunce, I've already found it,' said the crafty Bean. 'It's up in the wood on the hill. It's under a huge tree . . .'

Chapter Three

THE SHOOTING

'Well, my darling,' said Mr Fox. 'What shall it be tonight?'

'I think we'll have duck tonight,' said Mrs Fox.

'Bring us two fat ducks, if you please. One for you and me, and one for the children.'

'Ducks it shall be!' said Mr Fox. 'Bunce's best!'

'Now do be careful,' said Mrs Fox.

'My darling,' said Mr Fox, 'I can smell those goons a mile away. I can even smell one from the other. Boggis gives off a filthy stink of rotten chicken-skins. Bunce reeks of goose-livers, and as for Bean, the fumes of apple cider hang around him like poisonous gases.'

'Yes, but just don't get careless,' said Mrs Fox. 'You know they'll be

waiting for you, all three of them.'

'Don't you worry about me,' said Mr Fox. 'I'll see you later.'

But Mr Fox would not have been quite so cocky had he known exactly *where* the three farmers were waiting at that moment. They were just outside the entrance to the hole, each one crouching behind a tree with his gun loaded. And what is more, they had chosen their positions very carefully, making sure that the wind was not blowing from them towards the fox's hole. In fact, it was blowing in the opposite direction.

There was no chance of them being 'smelled out'.

Mr Fox crept up the dark tunnel to the mouth of his hole. He poked his long handsome face out into the night air and sniffed once.

He moved an inch or two forward and stopped.

He sniffed again. He was always especially careful when coming out from his hole.

He inched forward a little more. The front half of his body was now in the open.

His black nose twitched from side to side, sniffing and sniffing for the scent of danger. He found none, and he was just about to go trotting forward into the wood when he heard or thought he heard a tiny noise, a soft rustling sound, as though someone had moved a foot ever so gently through a patch of dry leaves.

Mr Fox flattened his body against the ground and lay very still, his ears pricked. He waited a long time, but he heard nothing more.

'It must have been a field-mouse,' he told himself, 'or some other small animal.'

He crept a little further out of the hole . . . then further still. He was almost right out in the open now. He took a last careful look around. The wood was murky and very still. Somewhere in the sky the moon was shining.

Just then, his sharp night-eyes caught a glint of something bright behind a tree not far away. It was a small silver speck of moonlight shining on a polished surface. Mr Fox lay still, watching it. What on earth was it? Now it was moving. It was coming up and up . . . *Great heavens! It was the barrel of a gun!* Quick as a whip, Mr Fox jumped back into his hole and at that same instant the entire wood seemed to explode around him. *Bang-bang! Bang-bang! Bang-bang!*

The smoke from the three guns floated upward in the night air. Boggis and

Bunce and Bean came out from behind their trees and walked towards the hole.

'Did we get him?' said Bean.

One of them shone a flashlight on the hole, and there on the ground, in the circle of light, half in and half out of the hole, lay the poor tattered bloodstained remains of . . . a fox's tail. Bean picked it up. 'We got the tail but we missed the fox,' he said, tossing the thing away.

'Dang and blast!' said Boggis. 'We shot too late. We should have let fly the moment he poked his head out.'

'He won't be poking it out again in a hurry,' Bunce said.

Bean pulled a flask from his pocket and took a swig of cider. Then he said, 'It'll take three days at least before he gets hungry enough to come out again. I'm not sitting around here waiting for that. Let's dig him out.'

'Ah,' said Boggis. 'Now you're talking sense. We can dig him out in a couple of hours. We know he's there.'

'I reckon there's a whole family of them down that hole,' Bunce said.

'Then we'll have the lot,' said Bean. 'Get the shovels!'

Chapter Four

THE TERRIBLE SHOVELS

Down the hole, Mrs Fox was tenderly licking the stump of Mr Fox's tail to stop the bleeding. 'It was the finest tail for miles around,' she said between licks.

'It hurts,' said Mr Fox.

'I know it does, sweetheart. But it'll soon get better.'

'And it will soon grow again, Dad,' said one of the Small Foxes.

'It will never grow again,' said Mr Fox. 'I shall be tail-less for the rest of my life.' He looked very glum.

There was no food for the foxes that night, and soon the children dozed off. Then Mrs Fox dozed off. But Mr Fox couldn't sleep because

of the pain in the stump of his tail. 'Well,' he thought, 'I suppose I'm lucky to be alive at all. And now they've found our hole, we're going to have to move out as soon as possible. We'll never get any peace if we . . . What was *that*?' He turned his head sharply and listened. The noise he heard now was the most frightening noise a fox can ever hear – the scrape-scrape-scraping of shovels digging into the soil.

'Wake up!' he shouted. 'They're digging us out!'

Mrs Fox was wide awake in one second. She sat up, quivering all over. 'Are you sure that's it?' she whispered.

'I'm positive! Listen!'

'They'll kill my children!' cried Mrs Fox.

'Never!' said Mr Fox.

'But darling, they will!' sobbed Mrs Fox. 'You know they will!'

Scrunch, scrunch, scrunch went the shovels above their heads. Small stones and bits of earth began falling from the roof of the tunnel.

'How will they kill us, Mummy?' asked one of the Small Foxes. His round black eyes were huge with fright. 'Will there be dogs?' he said.

Mrs Fox began to cry. She gathered her four children close to her and held them tight.

Suddenly there was an especially loud crunch above their heads and the sharp end of a shovel came right through the ceiling. The sight of this awful thing seemed to have an electric effect upon Mr Fox. He jumped up and shouted, 'I've got it! Come on! There's not a moment to lose! Why didn't I think of it before!'

'Think of what, Dad?'

'A fox can dig quicker than a man!' shouted Mr Fox, beginning to dig. 'Nobody in the world can dig as quick as a fox!'

The soil began to fly out furiously behind Mr Fox as he started to dig

for dear life with his front feet. Mrs Fox ran forward to help him. So did the four children.

'Go downwards!' ordered Mr Fox. 'We've got to go deep! As deep as we possibly can!'

The tunnel began to grow longer and longer. It sloped steeply downward. Deeper and deeper below the surface of the ground it went. The mother and the father and all four of the children were digging together. Their front legs were moving so fast you couldn't see them.

And gradually the scrunching and scraping of the shovels became fainter and fainter.

After about an hour, Mr Fox stopped digging. 'Hold it!' he said. They all stopped. They turned and looked back up the long tunnel they had just dug. All was quiet. 'Phew!' said Mr Fox. 'I think we've done it! They'll never get as deep as this. Well done, everyone!'

They all sat down, panting for breath. And Mrs Fox said to her children, 'I should like you to know that if it wasn't for your father we should all be dead by now. Your father is a fantastic fox.'

Mr Fox looked at his wife and she smiled. He loved her more than ever when she said things like that.

Chapter Five

THE TERRIBLE TRACTORS

As the sun rose the next morning, Boggis and Bunce and Bean were still digging. They had dug a hole so deep you could have put a house into it. But they had not yet come to the end of the foxes' tunnel. They were all very tired and cross.

'Dang and blast!' said Boggis. 'Whose rotten idea was this?'

'Bean's idea,' said Bunce.

Boggis and Bunce both stared at Bean. Bean took another swig of cider, then put the flask back into his pocket without offering it to the others. 'Listen,' he said angrily, 'I want that fox! I'm going to get that fox! I'm not giving in till I've strung him up over my front porch, dead as a dumpling!'

'We can't get him by digging, that's for sure,' said the fat Boggis. 'I've had enough of digging.'

Bunce, the little pot-bellied dwarf, looked up at Bean and said, 'Have you got any more stupid ideas, then?'

'What?' said Bean. 'I can't hear you.' Bean never took a bath. He never even washed. As a result, his earholes were clogged with all kinds of muck and wax and bits of chewing-gum and dead flies and stuff like that. This made him deaf. 'Speak louder,' he said to Bunce, and Bunce shouted back, 'Got any more stupid ideas?'

Bean rubbed the back of his neck

with a dirty finger. He had a boil coming there and it itched. 'What we need on this job,' he said, 'is machines . . . *mechanical* shovels. We'll have him out in five minutes with *mechanical* shovels.'

This was a pretty good idea and the other two had to admit it.

'All right then,' Bean said, taking charge. 'Boggis, you stay here and see the fox doesn't escape. Bunce and I will go and fetch our machinery. If he tries to get out, shoot him quick.'

The long, thin Bean walked away. The tiny Bunce trotted after him. The fat Boggis stayed where he was with his gun pointing at the fox-hole.

Soon, two enormous caterpillar tractors with mechanical shovels on their front ends came clanking into the wood. Bean was driving one. Bunce the other. The machines were both black. They were murderous, brutal-looking monsters.

'Here we go, then!' shouted Bean.

'Death to the fox!' shouted Bunce.

The machines went to work, biting huge mouthfuls of soil out of

the hill. The big tree under which Mr Fox had dug his hole in the first place was toppled like a matchstick. On all sides, rocks were sent flying and trees were falling and the noise was deafening.

Down in the tunnel the foxes crouched, listening to the terrible clanging and banging overhead. 'What's happening, Dad?' cried the Small Foxes. 'What are they doing?'

Mr Fox didn't know what was happening or what they were doing.

'It's an earthquake!' cried Mrs Fox.

'Look!' said one of the Small Foxes. 'Our tunnel's got shorter! I can see daylight!'

They all looked round, and yes, the mouth of the tunnel was only a

few feet away from them now, and in the circle of daylight beyond they could see the two huge black tractors almost on top of them.

'Tractors!' shouted Mr Fox. 'And *mechanical* shovels! Dig for your lives! *Dig, dig, dig!*'

Chapter Six

THE RACE

Now there began a desperate race, the machines against the foxes. In the beginning, the hill looked like this:

After about an hour, as the machines bit away more and more soil from the hilltop, it looked like this:

Sometimes the foxes would gain a little ground and the clanking noises would grow fainter and Mr Fox would say, 'We're going to make it! I'm sure we are!' But then a few moments later, the machines would come back at them and the crunch of the mighty shovels would get louder and louder. Once the foxes actually saw the sharp metal edge of one of the shovels as it scraped up the earth just behind them.

'Keep going, my darlings!' panted Mr Fox. 'Don't give up!'

'Keep going!' the fat Boggis shouted to Bunce and Bean. 'We'll get him any moment now!'

'Have you caught sight of him yet?' Bean called back.

'Not yet,' shouted Boggis. 'But I think you're close!'

'I'll pick him up with my bucket!' shouted Bunce. 'I'll chop him to pieces!'

But by lunchtime the machines were still at it. And so were the poor foxes. The hill now looked like this:

The farmers didn't stop for lunch; they were too keen to finish the job.

'Hey there, Mr Fox!' yelled Bunce, leaning out of his tractor. 'We're coming to get you now!'

'You've had your last chicken!' yelled Boggis. 'You'll never come prowling around *my* farm again!'

A sort of madness had taken hold of the three men. The tall skinny Bean and dwarfish pot-bellied Bunce were driving their machines like maniacs, racing the motors and making the shovels dig at a terrific speed. The fat Boggis was hopping about like a dervish and shouting, 'Faster! Faster!'

By five o'clock in the afternoon this is what had happened to the hill:

The hole the machines had dug was like the crater of a volcano. It was such an extraordinary sight that crowds of people came rushing out from the surrounding villages to have a look. They stood on the edge of the crater and stared down at Boggis and Bunce and Bean.

'Hey there, Boggis! What's going on?'

'We're after a fox!'

'You must be mad!'

The people jeered and laughed. But this only made the three farmers more furious and more obstinate and more determined than ever not to give up until they had caught the fox.

Chapter Seven

'We'll Never Let Him Go'

At six o'clock in the evening, Bean switched off the motor of his tractor and climbed down from the driver's seat. Bunce did the same. Both men had had enough. They were tired and stiff from driving the tractors all day. They were also hungry. Slowly they walked over to the small fox's hole in the bottom of the huge crater. Bean's face was purple with rage. Bunce was cursing the fox with dirty words that cannot be printed. Boggis came waddling up. 'Dang and blast that filthy stinking fox!' he said. 'What the heck do we do now?'

'I'll tell you what we *don't* do,' Bean said. 'We don't let him go!'

'We'll never let him go!' Bunce declared.

'Never never never!' cried Boggis.

'Did you hear that, Mr Fox!' yelled Bean, bending low and shouting down the hole. 'It's not over yet, Mr Fox! We're not going home till we've strung you up dead as a dingbat!' Whereupon the three men all shook hands with one another and swore a solemn oath that they would not go back to their farms until the fox was caught.

'What's the next move?' asked Bunce, the pot-bellied dwarf.

'We're sending you down the hole to fetch him up,' said Bean. 'Down you go, you miserable midget!'

'Not me!' screamed Bunce, running away.

Bean made a sickly smile. When he smiled you saw his scarlet gums. You saw more gums than teeth. 'Then there's only one thing to do,' he said. 'We starve him out. We camp here day and night watching the hole. He'll come out in the end. He'll have to.'

So Boggis and Bunce and Bean sent messages down to their farms asking for tents, sleeping-bags and supper.

Chapter Eight

THE FOXES BEGIN TO STARVE

That evening three tents were put up in the crater on the hill – one for Boggis, one for Bunce and one for Bean. The tents surrounded Mr Fox's hole. And the three farmers sat outside their tents eating their supper. Boggis had three boiled chickens smothered in dumplings, Bunce had six doughnuts filled with disgusting goose-liver paste, and Bean had two gallons of cider. All three of them kept their guns beside them.

Boggis picked up a steaming chicken and held it close to the fox's hole. 'Can you smell this, Mr Fox?' he shouted. 'Lovely tender chicken! Why don't you come up and get it?'

The rich scent of chicken wafted down the tunnel to where the foxes were crouching.

'Oh, Dad,' said one of the Small Foxes, 'couldn't we just sneak up and snatch it out of his hand?'

'Don't you dare!' said Mrs Fox. 'That's just what they want you to do.'

'But we're so *hungry!*' they cried. 'How long will it be till we get something to eat?'

Their mother didn't answer them. Nor did their father. There was no answer to give.

As darkness fell, Bunce and Bean switched on the powerful headlamps of the two tractors and shone them on to the hole. 'Now,' said Bean, 'we'll take it in turn to keep watch. One watches while two sleep, and so on all through the night.'

Boggis said, 'What if the fox digs a hole right through the hill and comes out on the other side? You didn't think of that one, did you?'

'Of course I did,' said Bean, pretending he had.

'Go on, then, tell us the answer,' said Boggis.

Bean picked something small and black out of his ear and flicked it away. 'How many men have you got working on your farm?' he asked.

'Thirty-five,' Boggis said.

'I've got thirty-six,' Bunce said.

'And I've got thirty-seven,' Bean said. 'That makes one hundred and eight men altogether. We must order them to surround the hill. Each man will have a gun and a flashlight. There will be no escape then for Mr Fox.'

So the order went down to the farms, and that night one hundred and eight men formed a tight ring around the bottom of the hill. They were armed with sticks and guns and hatchets and pistols and all sorts of other horrible weapons. This made it quite impossible for a fox or indeed for any other animal to escape from the hill.

The next day, the watching and waiting went on. Boggis and Bunce and Bean sat upon small stools, staring at the fox's hole. They didn't talk much. They just sat there with their guns on their laps.

Every so often, Mr Fox would creep a little closer towards the mouth of the tunnel and take a sniff. Then he would creep back again and say, 'They're still there.'

'Are you quite sure?' Mrs Fox would ask.

'Positive,' said Mr Fox. 'I can smell that man Bean a mile away. He stinks.'

Chapter Nine

MR FOX HAS A PLAN

For three days and three nights this waiting-game went on.

'How long can a fox go without food or water?' Boggis asked on the third day.

'Not much longer now,' Bean told him. 'He'll make a run for it soon. He'll have to.'

Bean was right. Down in the tunnel the foxes were slowly but surely starving to death.

'If only we could have just a tiny sip of water,' said one of the Small Foxes. 'Oh, Dad, can't you do *something*?'

'Couldn't we make a dash for it, Dad? We'd have a little bit of a chance, wouldn't we?'

'No chance at all,' snapped Mrs Fox. 'I refuse to let you go up there and face those guns. I'd sooner you stay down here and die in peace.'

Mr Fox had not spoken for a long time. He had been sitting quite still, his eyes closed, not even hearing what the others were saying. Mrs Fox knew that he was trying desperately to think of a way out. And now, as she looked at him, she saw him stir himself and get slowly to his feet. He looked back at his wife. There was a little spark of excitement dancing in his eyes.

'What is it, darling?' said Mrs Fox quickly.

'I've just had a bit of an idea,' Mr Fox said carefully.

'What?' they cried. 'Oh, Dad, what is it?'

'Come *on!*' said Mrs Fox. 'Tell us quickly!'

'Well . . .' said Mr Fox, then he stopped and sighed and sadly shook his head. He sat down again. 'It's no good,' he said. 'It won't work after all.'

'Why not, Dad?'

'Because it means more digging and we aren't any of us strong enough for that after three days and nights without food.'

'Yes we are, Dad!' cried the Small Foxes, jumping up and running to

their father. 'We can do it! You see if we can't! So can you!'

Mr Fox looked at the four Small Foxes and he smiled. What fine children I have, he thought. They are starving to death and they haven't had a drink for three days, but they are still undefeated. I must not let them down.

'I . . . I suppose we could give it a try,' he said.

'Let's go, Dad! Tell us what you want us to do!'

Slowly, Mrs Fox got to her feet. She was suffering more than any of them from the lack of food and water. She was very weak. 'I am so sorry,' she said, 'but I don't think I am going to be much help.'

'You stay right where you are, my darling,' said Mr Fox. 'We can handle this by ourselves.'

Chapter Ten

Boggis's Chicken House Number One

'This time we must go in a very special direction,' said Mr Fox, pointing sideways and downward.

So he and his four children started to dig once again. The work went much more slowly now. Yet they kept at it with great courage, and little by little the tunnel began to grow.

'Dad, I wish you would tell us *where* we are going,' said one of the children.

'I dare not do that,' said Mr Fox, 'because this place I am *hoping* to get to is so *marvellous* that if I described it to you now you would go crazy with excitement. And then, if we failed to get there (which is very possible), you would die of disappointment. I don't want to raise your hopes too much, my darlings.'

For a long long time they kept on digging. For how long they did not know, because there were no days and no nights down there in the murky tunnel. But at last Mr Fox gave the order to stop. 'I think,' he said, 'we had better take a peep upstairs now and see where we are. I know where I *want* to be, but I can't possibly be sure we're anywhere near it.'

Slowly, wearily, the foxes began to slope the tunnel up towards the surface. Up and up it went . . . until suddenly they came to something

hard above their heads and they couldn't go up any further. Mr Fox reached up to examine this hard thing. 'It's wood!' he whispered. 'Wooden planks!'

'What does that mean, Dad?'

'It means, unless I am very much mistaken, that we are right underneath somebody's house,' whispered Mr Fox. 'Be very quiet now while I take a peek.'

Carefully, Mr Fox began pushing up one of the floorboards.

The board creaked most terribly and they all ducked down, waiting for something awful to happen. Nothing did. So Mr Fox pushed up a second board. And then, very very cautiously, he poked his head up through the gap. He let out a shriek of excitement.

'*I've done it!*' he yelled. 'I've done it *first time! I've done it! I've done it!*' He pulled himself up through the gap in the floor and started prancing and dancing with joy. 'Come on up!' he sang out. 'Come up and see where you are, my darlings! What a sight for a hungry fox! Hallelujah! Hooray! Hooray!'

The four Small Foxes scrambled up out of the tunnel and what a fantastic sight it was that now met their eyes! They were in a huge shed and the whole place was teeming with chickens. There were white chickens and brown chickens and black chickens by the thousand!

'Boggis's Chicken House Number One!' cried Mr Fox. 'It's exactly what I was aiming at! I hit it slap in the middle! First time! Isn't that fantastic! *And*, if I may say so, rather clever!'

The Small Foxes went wild with excitement. They started running around in all directions, chasing the stupid chickens.

'Wait!' ordered Mr Fox. 'Don't lose your heads! Stand back! Calm down! Let's do this properly! First of all, everyone have a drink of water!'

They all ran over to the chickens' drinking-trough and lapped up the lovely cool water. Then Mr Fox chose three of the plumpest hens, and with a clever flick of his jaws he killed them instantly.

'Back to the tunnel!' he ordered. 'Come on! No fooling around! The quicker you move, the quicker you shall have something to eat!'

One after another, they climbed down through the hole in the floor and soon they were all standing once again in the dark tunnel. Mr Fox reached up and pulled the floorboards back into place. He did this with great care. He did it so that no one could tell they had ever been moved.

'My son,' he said, giving the three plump hens to the biggest of his four small children,

'run back with these to your mother. Tell her to prepare a feast. Tell her the rest of us will be along in a jiffy, as soon as we have made a few other little arrangements.'

Chapter Eleven

A Surprise for Mrs Fox

The Small Fox ran back along the tunnel as fast as he could, carrying the three plump hens. He was exploding with joy. 'Just wait!' he kept thinking, 'just wait till Mummy sees these!' He had a long way to run but he never stopped once on the way and he came bursting in upon Mrs Fox. 'Mummy!' he cried, out of breath. 'Look, Mummy, look! Wake up and see what I've brought you!'

Mrs Fox, who was weaker than ever now from lack of food, opened one eye and looked at the hens. 'I'm dreaming,' she murmured and closed the eye again.

'You're not dreaming, Mummy! They're real chickens! We're saved! We're not going to starve!'

Mrs Fox opened both eyes and sat up quickly. 'But, my *dear* child!' she cried. 'Where on earth . . .?'

'Boggis's Chicken House Number One!' spluttered the Small Fox. 'We tunnelled right up under the floor and you've never seen so many big fat hens in all your life! And Dad said to prepare a feast! They'll be back soon!'

The sight of food seemed to give new strength to Mrs Fox. 'A feast it shall be!' she said, standing up. 'Oh, what a fantastic fox your father is! Hurry up, child, and start plucking those chickens!'

Far away down in the tunnel, the fantastic Mr Fox was saying, 'Now for the next bit, my darlings! This one'll be as easy as pie! All we have to do is dig another little tunnel from *here* to there!'

'To where, Dad?'

'Don't ask so many questions. Start digging!'

Chapter Twelve

BADGER

Mr Fox and the three remaining Small Foxes dug fast and straight. They were all too excited now to feel tired or hungry. They knew they were going to have a whacking great feast before long and the fact that it was none other than Boggis's chickens they were going to eat made them churgle with laughter every time they thought of it. It was lovely to realize that while the fat farmer was sitting up there on the hill waiting for them to starve, he was also giving them their dinner without knowing it. 'Keep digging,' said Mr Fox. 'It's not much further.'

All of a sudden a deep voice above their heads said, '*Who goes there?*' The foxes jumped. They looked up quickly and they saw, peeking

through a small hole in the roof of the tunnel, a long black pointed furry face.

'Badger!' cried Mr Fox.

'Foxy!' cried Badger. 'My goodness me, I'm glad I've found *someone* at last! I've been digging around in circles for three days and nights and I haven't the foggiest idea where I am!'

Badger made the hole in the ceiling bigger and dropped down beside the foxes. A Small Badger (his son) dropped down after him. 'Haven't you *heard* what's happening up on the hill?' Badger said excitedly. 'It's chaos! Half the wood has disappeared and there are men with guns all over the countryside! None of us can get out, even at night! We're all starving to death!'

'Who is *we*?' asked Mr Fox.

'All us diggers. That's me and Mole and Rabbit and all our wives and children. Even Weasel, who can usually sneak out of the tightest spots, is right now hiding down my hole with Mrs Weasel and six kids. What on earth are we going to do, Foxy? I think we're finished!'

Mr Fox looked at his three children and he smiled. The children smiled back at him, sharing his secret. 'My dear old Badger,' he said, 'this mess you're in is all my fault . . .'

'I *know* it's your fault!' said Badger furiously. 'And the farmers are not going to give up till they've got you. Unfortunately, that means *us* as well. It means everyone on the hill.' Badger sat down and put a paw around his small son. 'We're done for,' he said softly. 'My poor wife up there is so weak she can't dig another yard.'

'Nor can mine,' said Mr Fox. 'And yet at this very minute she is preparing for me and my children the most delicious feast of plump juicy chickens . . .'

'Stop!' cried Badger. 'Don't tease me! I can't stand it!'

'It's true!' cried the Small Foxes. 'Dad's not teasing! We've got chickens galore!'

'And because everything is entirely my fault,' said Mr Fox, 'I invite you

to share the feast. I invite *everyone* to share it – you and Mole and Rabbit and Weasel and all your wives and children. There'll be plenty to go round, I can assure you.'

'You mean it?' cried Badger. 'You *really mean* it?'

Mr Fox pushed his face close to Badger's and whispered darkly, '*Do you know* where we've just been?'

'Where?'

'Right inside Boggis's Chicken House Number One!'

'No!'

'Yes! But that is nothing to where we are going now. You have come just at the right moment, my dear Badger. You can help us dig. And in the meanwhile, your small son can run back to Mrs Badger and all the others and spread the good news.' Mr Fox turned to the Small Badger and said, 'Tell them they are invited to a Fox's Feast. Then bring them all down here and follow this tunnel back until you find my home!'

'Yes, Mr Fox!' said the Small Badger. 'Yes, sir! Right away, sir! Oh, thank you, sir!' and he scrambled quickly back through the hole in the roof of the tunnel and disappeared.

Chapter Thirteen

BUNCE'S GIANT STOREHOUSE

'My dear Foxy!' cried Badger. 'What in the world has happened to your tail?'

'Don't talk about it, *please*,' said Mr Fox. 'It's a painful subject.'

They were digging the new tunnel. They dug on in silence. Badger was a great digger and the tunnel went forward at a terrific pace now that he was lending a paw. Soon they were crouching underneath yet another wooden floor.

Mr Fox grinned slyly, showing sharp white teeth. 'If I am not mistaken, my dear Badger,' he said, 'we are now underneath the farm which belongs to that nasty little pot-bellied dwarf, Bunce. We are, in fact, directly underneath the most *interesting part* of that farm.'

'Ducks and geese!' cried the Small Foxes, licking their lips. 'Juicy tender ducks and big fat geese!'

'Ex-*actly!*' said Mr Fox.

'But how in the world can you know where we are?' asked Badger.

Mr Fox grinned again, showing even more white teeth. 'Look,' he said, 'I know my way around these farms blindfold. For me it's just as easy below ground as it is above it.' He reached high and pushed up one wooden floorboard, then another. He poked his head through the gap.

'Yes!' he shouted, jumping up into the room above. 'I've done it again! I've hit it smack on the nose! Right in the bull's-eye! Come and look!'

Quickly Badger and the three Small Foxes scrambled up after him. They stopped and stared. They stood and gaped. They were so overwhelmed they couldn't speak; for what they now saw was a kind of fox's dream, a badger's dream, a paradise for hungry animals.

'This, my dear old Badger,' proclaimed Mr Fox, 'is Bunce's Mighty Storehouse! All his finest stuff is stored in here before he sends it off to market.'

Against all the four walls of the great room, stacked in cupboards and piled upon shelves reaching from floor to ceiling, were thousands and thousands of the finest and fattest ducks and geese, plucked and ready for roasting! And up above, dangling from the rafters, there must have been at least a hundred smoked hams and fifty sides of bacon!

'Just feast your eyes on *that!*' cried Mr Fox, dancing up and down. 'What d'you think of it, eh? Pretty good grub!'

Suddenly, as though springs had been released in their legs, the three hungry Small Foxes and the ravenously hungry Badger sprang forward to grab the luscious food.

'Stop!' ordered Mr Fox. 'This is *my* party, so *I* shall do the choosing.' The others fell back, licking their chops. Mr Fox began prowling around the storehouse examining the glorious display with an expert eye. A thread of saliva slid down one side of his jaw and hung suspended in mid-air, then snapped.

'We mustn't overdo it,' he said. 'Mustn't give the game away. Mustn't let them know what we've been up to. We must be neat and tidy and take just a few of the choicest morsels. So, to start with we shall have four plump young ducks.' He took them from the shelf. 'Oh, how lovely and fat they are! No wonder Bunce gets a special price for them in the market! . . . All

right, Badger, lend me a hand to get them down . . . You children can help as well . . . There we go . . . Goodness me, look how your mouths are watering . . . And now . . . I think we had better have a few geese . . . Three will be quite enough . . . We'll take the biggest . . . Oh my, oh my, you'll never see finer geese than these in a king's kitchen . . . Gently does it . . . that's the way . . . And what about a couple of nice smoked hams . . . I adore smoked ham, don't you, Badger? . . . Fetch me that step-ladder, will you please . . .'

Mr Fox climbed up the ladder and handed down three magnificent

hams. 'And do you like bacon, Badger?'

'I'm mad about bacon!' cried Badger, dancing with excitement. 'Let's have a side of bacon! That big one up there!'

'And carrots, Dad!' said the smallest of the three Small Foxes. 'We must take some of those carrots.'

'Don't be a twerp,' said Mr Fox. 'You know we never eat things like that.'

'It's not for us, Dad. It's for the Rabbits. They only eat vegetables.'

'My goodness me, you're right!' cried Mr Fox. 'What a thoughtful little fellow you are! Take ten bunches of carrots!'

Soon, all this lovely loot was lying in a neat heap upon the floor. The Small Foxes crouched close, their noses twitching, their eyes shining like stars.

'And now,' said Mr Fox, 'we shall have to borrow from our friend Bunce two of those useful push-carts over in the corner.' He and Badger fetched the push-carts, and the ducks and geese and hams and bacon were loaded on to them. Quickly the push-carts were lowered through the hole in the floor. The animals slid down after them. Back in the tunnel, Mr Fox again pulled the floorboards very carefully into place so that no one could see they had been moved.

'My darlings,' he said, pointing to two of the three Small Foxes, 'take a cart each and run back as fast as you can to your mother. Give her my love and tell her we are having guests for dinner – the Badgers, the Moles, the Rabbits and the Weasels. Tell her it must be a truly great feast. And tell her the rest of us will be home as soon as we've done one more little job.'

'Yes, Dad! Right away, Dad!' they answered, and they grabbed a trolley each and went rushing off down the tunnel.

Chapter Fourteen

BADGER HAS DOUBTS

'Just one more visit!' cried Mr Fox.

'And I'll bet I know where that'll be,' said the only Small Fox now left. He was the Smallest Fox of them all.

'Where?' asked Badger.

'Well,' said the Smallest Fox. 'We've been to Boggis and we've been to Bunce but we haven't been to Bean. It must be Bean.'

'You are right,' said Mr Fox. 'But what you don't know is which *part* of Bean's place we are about to visit.'

'Which?' they said both together.

'Ah-ha,' said Mr Fox. 'Just you wait and see.' They were digging as they talked. The tunnel was going forward fast.

Suddenly Badger said, 'Doesn't this worry you just a tiny bit, Foxy?'

'Worry me?' said Mr Fox. 'What?'

'All this . . . this *stealing*.'

Mr Fox stopped digging and stared at Badger as though he had gone completely dotty. 'My dear old furry frump,' he said, 'do you know anyone in the *whole world* who wouldn't swipe a few chickens if his children were starving to death?'

There was a short silence while Badger thought deeply about this.

'You are far too respectable,' said Mr Fox.

'There's nothing wrong with being respectable,' Badger said.

'Look,' said Mr Fox, 'Boggis and Bunce and Bean are out to *kill* us. You realize that, I hope?'

'I do, Foxy, I do indeed,' said the gentle Badger.

'But *we're* not going to stoop to *their* level. We don't want to kill *them.*'

'I should hope not, indeed,' said Badger.

'We wouldn't dream of it,' said Mr Fox. 'We shall simply take a little food here and there to keep us and our families alive. Right?'

'I suppose we'll have to,' said Badger.

'If *they* want to be horrible, let them,' said Mr Fox. 'We down here are decent peace-loving people.'

Badger laid his head on one side and smiled at Mr Fox. 'Foxy,' he said, 'I love you.'

'Thank you,' said Mr Fox. 'And now let's get on with the digging.'

Five minutes later, Badger's front paws hit against something flat and hard. 'What on earth is this?' he said. 'It looks like a solid stone wall.' He and Mr Fox scraped away the soil. It *was* a wall. But it was built of bricks, not stones. The wall was right in front of them, blocking their way.

'Now who in the world would build a wall under the ground?' asked Badger.

'Very simple,' said Mr Fox. 'It's the wall of an underground room. And if I am not mistaken, it is exactly what I'm looking for.'

Chapter Fifteen

Bean's Secret Cider Cellar

Mr Fox examined the wall carefully. He saw that the cement between the bricks was old and crumbly, so he loosened a brick without much trouble and pulled it away. Suddenly, out from the hole where the brick had been, there popped a small sharp face with whiskers, 'Go away!' it snapped. 'You can't come in here! It's private!'

'Good Lord!' said Badger. 'It's Rat!'

'You saucy beast!' said Mr Fox. 'I should have guessed we'd find you down here somewhere.'

'Go away!' shrieked Rat. 'Go on, beat it! This is my private pitch!'

'Shut up,' said Mr Fox.

'I will not shut up!' shrieked Rat. 'This is *my* place! I got here first!'

Mr Fox gave a brilliant smile, flashing his white teeth. 'My dear Rat,'

he said softly, 'I am a hungry fellow and if you don't hop it quickly I shall eat-you-up-in-one-gulp!'

That did it. Rat popped back fast out of sight. Mr Fox laughed and began pulling more bricks out of the wall. When he had made a biggish hole, he crept through it. Badger and the Smallest Fox followed him in.

They found themselves in a vast, damp, gloomy cellar. 'This is it!' cried Mr Fox.

'This is *what*?' said Badger. 'The place is empty.'

'Where are the turkeys?' asked the Smallest Fox, staring into the gloom. 'I thought Bean was a turkey man.'

'He is a turkey man,' said Mr Fox. 'But we're not after turkeys now. We've got plenty of food.'

'Then what *do* we need, Dad?'

'Take a good look round,' said Mr Fox. 'Don't you see *anything* that interests you?'

Badger and the Smallest Fox peered into the half-darkness. As their eyes became accustomed to the gloom, they began to see what looked like a whole lot of big glass jars standing upon shelves around the walls. They went closer. They *were* jars. There were hundreds of them, and upon each one was written the word CIDER.

The Smallest Fox leaped high in the air. 'Oh, Dad!' he cried out. 'Look what we've found! It's cider!'

'Ex-*actly*,' said Mr Fox.

'Tremendous!' shouted Badger.

'Bean's Secret Cider Cellar,' said Mr Fox. 'But go carefully, my dears. Don't make a noise. This cellar is right underneath the farmhouse itself.'

'Cider,' said Badger, 'is especially good for Badgers. We take it as medicine – one large glass three times a day with meals and another at bedtime.'

'It will make the feast into a banquet,' said Mr Fox.

While they were talking, the Smallest Fox had sneaked a jar off the shelf and had taken a gulp. 'Wow!' he gasped. 'Wow-*ee!*'

You must understand this was not the ordinary weak fizzy cider one buys in a store. It was the real stuff, a home-brewed fiery liquor that burned in your throat and boiled in your stomach.

'Ah-h-h-h-h-h!' gasped the Smallest Fox. 'This is *some cider!*'

'That's quite enough of that,' said Mr Fox, grabbing the jar and putting it to his own lips. He took a tremendous gulp. 'It's miraculous!' he whispered, fighting for breath. 'It's fabulous! It's beautiful!'

'It's my turn,' said Badger, taking the jar and tilting his head well back. The cider gurgled and bubbled down his throat. 'It's . . . it's like

melted gold!' he gasped. 'Oh, Foxy, it's . . . like drinking sunbeams and rainbows!'

'You're poaching!' shrieked Rat. 'Put that down at once! There'll be none left for me!' Rat was perched upon the highest shelf in the cellar, peering out from behind a huge jar. There was a small rubber tube inserted in the neck of the jar, and Rat was using this tube to suck out the cider.

'You're drunk!' said Mr Fox.

'Mind your own business!' shrieked Rat. 'And if you great clumsy brutes come messing about in here we'll all be caught! Get out and leave me to sip my cider in peace.'

At that moment they heard a woman's voice calling out in the house above them. 'Hurry up and get that cider, Mabel!' the voice called. 'You know Mr Bean doesn't like to be kept waiting! Especially when he's been out all night in a tent!'

The animals froze. They stayed absolutely still, their ears pricked, their bodies tense. Then they heard the sound of a door being opened. The door was at the top of a flight of stone steps leading down from the house to the cellar.

And now someone was starting to come down those steps.

Chapter Sixteen

THE WOMAN

'Quick!' said Mr Fox. 'Hide!' He and Badger and the Smallest Fox jumped up on to a shelf and crouched behind a row of big cider jars. Peering around the jars, they saw a huge woman coming down into the cellar. At the foot of the steps, the woman paused, looking to right and left. Then she turned and headed straight for the place where Mr Fox and Badger and the Smallest Fox were hiding. She stopped right in front of them. The only thing between her and them was a row of cider jars. She was so close, Mr Fox could hear the sound of her breathing. Peeping through the crack between two bottles, he noticed that she carried a big rolling-pin in one hand.

'How many will he want this time, Mrs Bean?' the woman shouted. And from the top of the steps the other voice called back, 'Bring up two or three jars.'

'He drank four yesterday, Mrs Bean.'

'Yes, but he won't want that many today because he's not going to be up there more than a few hours longer. He says the fox is bound to make a run for it this morning. It can't possibly stay down that hole another day without food.'

The woman in the cellar reached out and lifted a jar of cider from the shelf. The jar she took was next but one to the jar behind which Mr Fox was crouching.

'I'll be glad when the rotten brute is killed and strung up on the front porch,' she called out. 'And by the way, Mrs Bean, your husband promised I could have the tail as a souvenir.'

'The tail's been all shot to pieces,' said the voice from upstairs. 'Didn't you know that?'

'You mean it's *ruined*?'

'Of course it's ruined. They shot the tail but missed the fox.'

'Oh heck!' said the big woman. 'I did so want that tail!'

'You can have the head instead, Mabel. You can get it stuffed and hang it on your bedroom wall. Hurry up now with that cider!'

'Yes, Ma'am, I'm coming,' said the big woman, and she took a second jar from the shelf.

If she takes one more, she'll see us, thought Mr Fox. He could feel the Smallest Fox's body pressed tightly against his own, quivering with excitement.

'Will two be enough, Mrs Bean, or shall I take three?'

'My goodness, Mabel, I don't care so long as you get a move on!'

'Then two it is,' said the huge woman, speaking to herself now. 'He drinks too much anyway.'

Carrying a jar in each hand and with the rolling-pin tucked under one arm, she walked away across the cellar. At the foot of the steps she paused and looked around, sniffing the air. 'There's rats down here again, Mrs Bean. I can smell 'em.'

'Then poison them, woman, poison them! You know where the poison's kept.'

'Yes, Ma'am,' Mabel said. She climbed slowly out of sight up the steps. The door slammed.

'Quick!' said Mr Fox. 'Grab a jar each and run for it!'

Rat stood on his high shelf and shrieked. 'What did I tell you! You nearly got nabbed, didn't you? You nearly gave the game away!

You keep out of here from now on! I don't want you around! This is my place!'

'*You*,' said Mr Fox, 'are going to be poisoned.'

'Poppycock!' said Rat. 'I sit up here and watch her putting the stuff down. She'll never get *me*.'

Mr Fox and Badger and the Smallest Fox ran across the cellar clutching a gallon jar each. 'Goodbye, Rat!' they called out as they disappeared through the hole in the wall. 'Thanks for the lovely cider!'

'Thieves!' shrieked Rat. 'Robbers! Bandits! Burglars!'

Chapter Seventeen

THE GREAT FEAST

Back in the tunnel they paused so that Mr Fox could brick up the hole in the wall. He was humming to himself as he put the bricks back in place. 'I can still taste that glorious cider,' he said. 'What an impudent fellow Rat is.'

'He has bad manners,' Badger said. 'All rats have bad manners. I've never met a polite rat yet.'

'And he drinks too much,' said Mr Fox, putting the last brick in place. 'There we are. Now, home to the feast!'

They grabbed their jars of cider and off they went. Mr Fox was in front, the Smallest Fox came next and Badger last. Along the tunnel they flew . . . past the turning that led to Bunce's Mighty Storehouse . . . past Boggis's Chicken House Number One and then up the long home

stretch towards the place where they knew Mrs Fox would be waiting.

'Keep it up, my darlings!' shouted Mr Fox. 'We'll soon be there! Think what's waiting for us at the other end! And just think what we're bringing home with us in these jars! That ought to cheer up poor Mrs Fox.' Mr Fox sang a little song as he ran:

'Home again swiftly I glide,
Back to my beautiful bride.
She'll not feel so rotten
As soon as she's gotten
Some cider inside her inside.'

Then Badger joined in:

'Oh poor Mrs Badger, he cried,
So hungry she very near died.
But she'll not feel so hollow
If only she'll swallow
Some cider inside her inside.'

They were still singing as they rounded the final corner and burst in upon the most wonderful and amazing sight any of them had ever seen. The feast was just beginning. A large dining-room had been hollowed out of the earth, and in the middle of it, seated around a huge table, were no less than twenty-nine animals. They were:

Mrs Fox and three Small Foxes.

Mrs Badger and three Small Badgers.

Mole and Mrs Mole and four Small Moles.

Rabbit and Mrs Rabbit and five Small Rabbits.

Weasel and Mrs Weasel and six Small Weasels.

The table was covered with chickens and ducks and geese and hams and bacon, and everyone was tucking into the lovely food.

'My darling!' cried Mrs Fox, jumping up and hugging Mr Fox. 'We couldn't wait! Please forgive us!' Then she hugged the Smallest Fox of all, and Mrs Badger hugged Badger, and everyone hugged everyone else. Amid shouts of joy, the great jars of cider were placed upon the table, and Mr Fox and Badger and the Smallest Fox sat down with the others.

You must remember no one had eaten a thing for several days. They were ravenous. So for a while there was no conversation at all. There was only the sound of crunching and chewing as the animals attacked the succulent food.

At last, Badger stood up. He raised his glass of cider and called out, 'A toast! I want you all to stand and drink a toast to our dear friend who has saved our lives this day – Mr Fox!'

'To Mr Fox!' they all shouted, standing up and raising their glasses. 'To Mr Fox! Long may he live!'

Then Mrs Fox got shyly to her feet and said, 'I don't want to make a speech. I just want to say one thing, and it is this: MY HUSBAND IS

A FANTASTIC FOX.' Everyone clapped and cheered. Then Mr Fox himself stood up.

'This delicious meal . . .' he began, then he stopped. In the silence that followed, he let fly a tremendous belch. There was laughter and more

clapping. 'This delicious meal, my friends,' he went on, 'is by courtesy of Messrs Boggis, Bunce and Bean.' (More cheering and laughter.) 'And I hope you have enjoyed it as much as I have.' He let fly another colossal belch.

'Better out than in,' said Badger.

'Thank you,' said Mr Fox, grinning hugely. 'But now, my friends, let us be serious. Let us think of tomorrow and the next day and the days after that. If we go out, we will be killed. Right?'

'Right!' they shouted.

'We'll be shot before we've gone a yard,' said Badger.

'Ex-*actly*,' said Mr Fox. 'But who *wants* to go out, anyway; let me ask you that? We are all diggers, every one of us. We hate the outside. The outside is full of enemies. We only go out because we have to, to get food for our families. But now, my friends, we have an entirely new set-up. We have a safe tunnel leading to three of the finest stores in the world!'

'We do indeed!' said Badger. 'I've seen 'em!'

'And you know what this means?' said Mr Fox. *'It means that none of us need ever go out into the open again!'*

There was a buzz of excitement around the table.

'I therefore invite you all,' Mr Fox went on, 'to stay here with me for ever.'

'For ever!' they cried. 'My goodness! How marvellous!' And Rabbit said to Mrs Rabbit, 'My dear, just think! We're never going to be shot at again in our lives!'

'We will make,' said Mr Fox, 'a little underground village, with streets and houses on each side – separate houses for Badgers and Moles and

Rabbits and Weasels and Foxes. And every day I will go shopping for you all. And every day we will eat like kings.'

The cheering that followed this speech went on for many minutes.

Chapter Eighteen

STILL WAITING

Outside the fox's hole, Boggis and Bunce and Bean sat beside their tents with their guns on their laps. It was beginning to rain. Water was trickling down the necks of the three men and into their shoes.

'He won't stay down there much longer now,' Boggis said.

'The brute must be famished,' Bunce said.

'That's right,' Bean said. 'He'll be making a dash for it any moment. Keep your guns handy.'

They sat there by the hole, waiting for the fox to come out.

And so far as I know, they are still waiting.

The Enormous Crocodile

To Sophie

R.D.

In the biggest brownest muddiest river in Africa, two crocodiles lay with their heads just above the water. One of the crocodiles was enormous. The other was not so big.

"Do you know what I would like for my lunch today?" the Enormous Crocodile asked.

"No," the Notsobig One said. "What?"

The Enormous Crocodile grinned, showing hundreds of sharp white teeth. "For my lunch today," he said, "I would like a nice juicy little child."

"I never eat children," the Notsobig One said. "Only fish."

"Ho, ho, ho!" cried the Enormous Crocodile. "I'll bet if you saw a fat juicy little child paddling in the water over there at this very moment, you'd gulp him up in one gollop!"

"No, I wouldn't," the Notsobig One said. "Children are too tough and chewy. They are tough and chewy and nasty and bitter."

"*Tough* and *chewy*!" cried the Enormous Crocodile. "*Nasty* and *bitter*! What awful tommy-rot you talk! They are juicy and yummy!"

"They taste so bitter," the Notsobig One said, "you have to cover them with sugar before you can eat them."

"Children are bigger than fish," said the Enormous Crocodile. "You get bigger helpings."

"You are greedy," the Notsobig One said. "You're the greediest croc in the whole river."

"I'm the bravest croc in the whole river," said the Enormous Crocodile. "I'm the only one who dares to leave the water and go through the jungle to the town to look for little children to eat."

"You've only done that once," snorted the Notsobig One. "And what happened then? They all saw you coming and ran away."

"Ah, but today when I go, they won't see me at all," said the Enormous Crocodile.

"Of course they'll see you," the Notsobig One said. "You're so enormous and ugly, they'll see you from miles away."

The Enormous Crocodile grinned again, and his terrible sharp teeth sparkled like knives in the sun. "Nobody will see me," he said, "because this time I've thought up secret plans and clever tricks."

"*Clever tricks?*" cried the Notsobig One. "You've never done anything clever in your life! You're the stupidest croc on the whole river!"

"I'm the cleverest croc on the whole river," the Enormous Crocodile answered. "For my lunch today I shall feast upon a fat juicy little child while you lie here in the river feeling hungry. Goodbye."

The Enormous Crocodile swam to the side of the river, and crawled out of the water.

A gigantic creature was standing in the slimy oozy mud on the river-bank. It was Humpy-Rumpy, the Hippopotamus.

"Hello, hello," said Humpy-Rumpy. "Where on earth are you off to at this time of day?"

"I have secret plans and clever tricks," said the Crocodile.

"Oh dear," said Humpy-Rumpy. "I'll bet you're going to do something horrid."

The Enormous Crocodile grinned at Humpy-Rumpy and said:

"I'm going to fill my hungry empty tummy
With something yummy yummy yummy yummy!"

"What's so yummy?" asked Humpy-Rumpy.

"Try to guess," said the Crocodile. "It's something that walks on two legs."

"You don't mean . . ." said Humpy-Rumpy. "You don't *really* mean you're going to eat a little child?"

"Of course I am," said the Crocodile.

"Oh, you horrid greedy grumptious brute!" cried Humpy-Rumpy. "I hope you get caught and cooked and turned into crocodile soup!"

The Enormous Crocodile laughed out loud at Humpy-Rumpy. Then he waddled off into the jungle.

Inside the jungle, he met Trunky, the Elephant. Trunky was nibbling leaves from the top of a tall tree, and he didn't notice the Crocodile at first. So the Crocodile bit him on the leg.

"Ow!" said Trunky in his big deep voice. "Who did that? Oh, it's you, is it, you beastly Crocodile. Why don't you go back to the big brown muddy river where you belong?"

"I have secret plans and clever tricks," said the Crocodile.

"You mean you've *nasty* plans and *nasty* tricks," said Trunky. "You've never done a nice thing in your life."

The Enormous Crocodile grinned up at Trunky and said:

"I'm off to find a yummy child for lunch.
Keep listening and you'll hear the bones go crunch!"

"Oh, you wicked beastly beast!" cried Trunky. "Oh, you foul and filthy fiend! I hope you get squashed and squished and squizzled and boiled up into crocodile stew!"

The Enormous Crocodile laughed out loud and disappeared into the thick jungle.

A bit further on, he met Muggle-Wump, the Monkey. Muggle-Wump was sitting in a tree, eating nuts.

"Hello, Crocky," said Muggle-Wump. "What are you up to now?"

"I have secret plans and clever tricks," said the Crocodile.

"Would you like some nuts?" asked Muggle-Wump.

"I have better things to eat than nuts," sniffed the Crocodile.

"I didn't think there *was* anything better than nuts," said Muggle-Wump.

"Ah-ha," said the Enormous Crocodile,

"The sort of things that I'm going to eat
Have fingers, toe-nails, arms and legs and feet!"

Muggle-Wump went pale and began to shake all over. "You aren't really going to gobble up a little child, are you?" he said.

"Of course I am," said the Crocodile. "Clothes and all. They taste better with the clothes on."

"Oh, you horrid hoggish croc!" cried Muggle-Wump. "You slimy creature! I hope the buttons and buckles all stick in your throat and choke you to death!"

The Crocodile grinned up at Muggle-Wump and said, "I eat monkeys, too." And quick as a flash, with one bite of his huge jaws, he bit through the tree that Muggle-Wump was sitting in, and down it came.

But just in time, Muggle-Wump jumped into the next tree and swung away through the branches.

A bit further on, the Enormous Crocodile met the Roly-Poly Bird. The Roly-Poly Bird was building a nest in an orange tree.

"Hello there, Enormous Crocodile!" sang the Roly-Poly Bird. "We don't often see you up here in the jungle."

"Ah," said the Crocodile. "I have secret plans and clever tricks."

"I hope it's not something nasty," sang the Roly-Poly Bird.

"*Nasty!*" cried the Crocodile. "Of course it's not nasty! It's delicious."

"It's luscious, it's super,
It's mushious, it's duper,
It's better than rotten old fish.
You mash it and munch it,
You chew it and crunch it!
It's lovely to hear it go squish!"

"It must be berries," sang the Roly-Poly Bird. "Berries are my favourite food in the world. Is it raspberries, perhaps? Or could it be strawberries?"

The Enormous Crocodile laughed so much his teeth rattled together like pennies in a moneybox.

"Crocodiles don't eat berries," he said. "We eat little boys and girls. And sometimes we eat Roly-Poly Birds, as well." Very quickly, the Crocodile reached up and snapped his jaws at the Roly-Poly Bird. He just missed the Bird, but he managed to catch hold of the long beautiful feathers in its tail. The Roly-Poly Bird gave a shriek of terror and shot straight up into the air, leaving its tail feathers behind in the Enormous Crocodile's mouth.

At last, the Enormous Crocodile came out of the other side of the jungle into the sunshine. He could see the town not far away.

"Ho-ho!" he said, talking aloud to himself. "Ha-ha! That walk through the jungle has made me hungrier than ever. One child isn't going to be nearly enough for me today. I won't be full up until I've eaten at least three juicy little children!"

He started to creep forward towards the town.

The Enormous Crocodile crept over to a place where there were a lot of coconut trees.

He knew that children from the town often came here looking for coconuts. The trees were too tall for them to climb, but there were always some coconuts on the ground that had fallen down.

The Enormous Crocodile quickly collected all the coconuts that were lying on the ground. He also gathered together several fallen branches.

"Now for Clever Trick Number One!" he whispered to himself. "It won't be long before I am eating the first part of my lunch!"

He took all the coconut branches and held them between his teeth.

He grasped the coconuts in his front paws. Then he stood straight up in the air, balancing himself on his tail.

He arranged the branches and the coconuts so cleverly that he now looked exactly like a small coconut tree standing among the big coconut trees.

Soon, two children came along. They were brother and sister. The boy was called Toto. His sister was called Mary. They walked around looking for fallen coconuts, but they couldn't find any because the Enormous Crocodile had gathered them all up.

"Oh look!" cried Toto. "That tree over there is much smaller than the others! And it's full of coconuts! I think I could climb that one quite easily if you help me up the first bit."

Toto and Mary ran towards what they thought was the small coconut tree.

The Enormous Crocodile peered through the branches, watching them as they came closer and closer. He licked his lips. He began to dribble with excitement.

Suddenly there was a tremendous whooshing noise. It was Humpy-Rumpy, the Hippopotamus. He came crashing and snorting out of the jungle. His head was down low and he was galloping at a terrific speed.

"Look out, Toto!" shouted Humpy-Rumpy. "Look out, Mary! That's not a coconut tree! It's the Enormous Crocodile and he wants to eat you up!"

Humpy-Rumpy charged straight at the Enormous Crocodile. He caught him with his giant head and sent him tumbling and skidding over the ground.

"Ow-eeee!" cried the Crocodile. "Help! Stop! Where am I?"

Toto and Mary ran back to the town as fast as they could.

But crocodiles are tough. It is difficult for even a Hippopotamus to hurt them.

The Enormous Crocodile picked himself up and crept towards the place where the children's playground was.

"Now for Clever Trick Number Two!" he said to himself. "This one is certain to work!"

There were no children in the playground at that moment. They were all in school.

The Enormous Crocodile found a large piece of wood and placed it in the middle of the playground. Then he lay across the piece of wood and tucked in his feet so that he looked almost exactly like a see-saw.

When school was over, the children all came running on to the playground.

"Oh look!" they cried. "We've got a new see-saw!"

They all crowded round, shouting with excitement.

"Bags I have the first go!"

"I'll get on the other end!"

"I want to go first!"

"So do I! So do I!"

Then, a girl who was older than the others said, "It's rather a funny knobbly sort of a see-saw, isn't it? Do you think it'll be safe to sit on?"

"Of course it will!" the others said. "It looks strong as anything!"

The Enormous Crocodile opened one eye just a tiny bit and watched the children who were crowding around him. Soon, he thought, one of them is going to sit on my head, then I will give a jerk and a snap, and after that it will be *yum yum yum*.

At that moment, there was a flash of brown and something jumped into the playground and hopped up on to the top of the swings.

It was Muggle-Wump, the Monkey.

"Run!" Muggle-Wump shouted to the children. "All of you, run, run, run! That's not a see-saw! It's the Enormous Crocodile and he wants to eat you up!"

The children screamed and ran for their lives.

Muggle-Wump disappeared back into the jungle, and the Enormous Crocodile was left all alone in the playground.

He cursed the Monkey and waddled back into the bushes to hide.

"I'm getting hungrier and hungrier!" he said. "I shall have to eat at least four children now before I am full up!"

The Enormous Crocodile crept around the edge of the town, taking great care not to be seen.

He came to a place where they were getting ready to have a fair. There were slides and swings and dodgem-cars and people selling popcorn and candy-floss. There was also a big roundabout.

The roundabout had marvellous wooden creatures for the children to ride on. There were white horses and lions and tigers and mermaids with fishes' tails and fearsome dragons with red tongues sticking out of their mouths.

"Now for Clever Trick Number Three," said the Enormous Crocodile, licking his lips.

When no one was looking, he crept up on to the roundabout and put himself between a wooden lion and a fearsome dragon. He sat up a bit on his back legs and he kept very still. He looked exactly like a wooden crocodile on the roundabout.

Soon, all sorts of children came flocking into the fair. Several of them ran towards the roundabout. They were very excited.

"I'm going to ride on a dragon!" cried one.

"I'm going on a lovely white horse!" cried another.

"I'm going on a lion!" cried a third one.

And one little girl, whose name was Jill said, "*I'm* going to ride on that funny old wooden crocodile!"

The Enormous Crocodile kept very still, but he could see the little girl coming towards him. "Yummy-yum-yum," he thought. "I'll gulp her up easily in one gollop."

Suddenly there was a *swish* and a *swoosh* and something came swishing and swooshing out of the sky.

It was the Roly-Poly Bird.

He flew round and round the roundabout, singing, "Look out, Jill! Look out! Look out! Don't ride on that crocodile!"

Jill stopped and looked up.

"That's not a wooden crocodile!" sang the Roly-Poly Bird. "It's a real one! It's the Enormous Crocodile from the river and he wants to eat you up!"

Jill turned and ran. So did all the other children. Even the man who was working the roundabout jumped off it and ran away as fast as he could.

The Enormous Crocodile cursed the Roly-Poly Bird and waddled back into the bushes to hide.

"I'm so hungry now," he said to himself, "I could eat six children before I am full up!"

Just outside the town, there was a pretty little field with trees and bushes all round it. This was called The Picnic Place. There were several wooden tables and long benches, and people were allowed to go there and have a picnic at any time.

The Enormous Crocodile crept over to The Picnic Place. There was no one in sight.

"Now for Clever Trick Number Four!" he whispered to himself.

He picked a lovely bunch of flowers and arranged it on one of the tables.

From the same table, he took away one of the benches and hid it in the bushes.

Then he put himself in the place where the bench had been.

By tucking his head under his chest, and by twisting his tail out of sight, he made himself look very much like a long wooden bench with four legs.

Soon, two boys and two girls came along carrying baskets of food. They were all from one family, and their mother had said they could go out and have a picnic together.

"Which table shall we sit at?" said one.

"Let's take the table with the lovely flowers on it," said another.

The Enormous Crocodile kept as quiet as a mouse. "I shall eat them all," he said to himself. "They will come and sit on my back and I will swizzle my head around quickly, and after that it'll be *squish crunch gollop.*"

Suddenly a big deep voice from the jungle shouted, "Stand back, children! Stand back! Stand back!"

The children stopped and stared at the place where the voice was coming from.

Then, with a crashing of branches, Trunky the Elephant came rushing out of the jungle.

"That's not a bench you were going to sit on!" he bellowed. "It's the Enormous Crocodile, and he wants to eat you all up!"

Trunky trotted over to the spot where the Enormous Crocodile was standing, and quick as a flash he wrapped his trunk around the Crocodile's tail and hoisted him up into the air.

"Hey! Let me go!" yelled the Enormous Crocodile, who was now dangling upside down. "Let me go! Let me go!"

"No," Trunky said. "I will not let you go. We've all had quite enough of your clever tricks."

Trunky began to swing the Crocodile round and round in the air. At first he swung him slowly.

Then he swung him faster . . .

And FASTER . . .

And FASTER . . .

And FASTER STILL . . .

Soon the Enormous Crocodile was just a blurry circle going round and round Trunky's head.

Suddenly, Trunky let go of the Crocodile's tail, and the Crocodile went shooting high up into the sky like a huge green rocket.
Up and up he went . . .

HIGHER

and

HIGHER . . .

FASTER

and

FASTER . . .

He was going so fast and so high that soon the earth was just a tiny dot miles below.

He whizzed on and on.
He whizzed far into space.
He whizzed past the moon.
He whizzed past stars and planets.
Until at last . . .

With the most tremendous

BANG!

the Enormous Crocodile crashed
headfirst into the hot hot sun.

And he was sizzled up like a sausage!

The Giraffe and the Pelly and Me

For Neisha, Charlotte and Lorina

Not far from where I live there is a queer old empty wooden house standing all by itself on the side of the road. I long to explore inside it but the door is always locked, and when I peer through a window all I can see is darkness and dust. I know the ground floor used once to be a shop because I can still read the faded lettering across the front which says THE GRUBBER. My mother has told me that in our part of the country in the olden days a grubber was another name for a sweet-shop, and now every time I look at it I think to myself what a lovely old sweet-shop it must have been.

On the shop-window itself somebody has painted in white the words FOR SAIL.

One morning, I noticed that FOR SAIL had been scraped off the shop-window and in its place somebody had painted SOLED. I stood there staring at the new writing and wishing like mad that it had been me who had bought it because then I would have been able to make it into a grubber all over again. I have always longed and longed to own a sweet-shop. The sweet-shop of my dreams would be loaded from top to bottom with Sherbet Suckers and Caramel Fudge and Russian Toffee and Sugar Snorters and Butter Gumballs and thousands and thousands of other glorious things like that. Oh boy, what I couldn't have done with that old Grubber shop if it had been mine!

On my next visit to The Grubber, I was standing across the road gazing at the wonderful old building when suddenly an enormous bathtub came sailing out through one of the second-floor windows and crashed right on to the middle of the road!

A few moments later, a white porcelain lavatory pan with the wooden seat still on it came flying out of the same window and landed with a wonderful splintering crash just beside the bath-tub. This was followed by a kitchen sink and an empty canary-cage and a four-poster bed and two hot-water bottles and a rocking horse and a sewing-machine and goodness knows what else besides.

It looked as though some madman was ripping out the whole of the inside of the house, because now pieces of staircase and bits of the banisters and a whole lot of old floorboards came whistling through the windows.

Then there was silence. I waited and waited but not another sound came from within the building. I crossed the road and stood right under the windows and called out, "Is anybody at home?" There was no answer.

In the end it began to get dark so I had to turn away and start walking home. But you can bet your life nothing was going to stop me from hurrying back there again tomorrow morning to see what the next surprise was going to be.

When I got back to the Grubber house the next morning, the first thing I noticed was the new door. The dirty old brown door had been taken out and in its place someone had fitted a brand-new red one. The new door was fantastic. It was twice as high as the other one had been and it looked ridiculous. I couldn't begin to imagine who would want a tremendous tall door like that in his house unless it was a giant.

As well as this, somebody had scraped away the SOLED notice on the shop-window and now there was a whole lot of different writing all over the glass. I stood there reading it and reading it and trying to figure out what on earth it all meant.

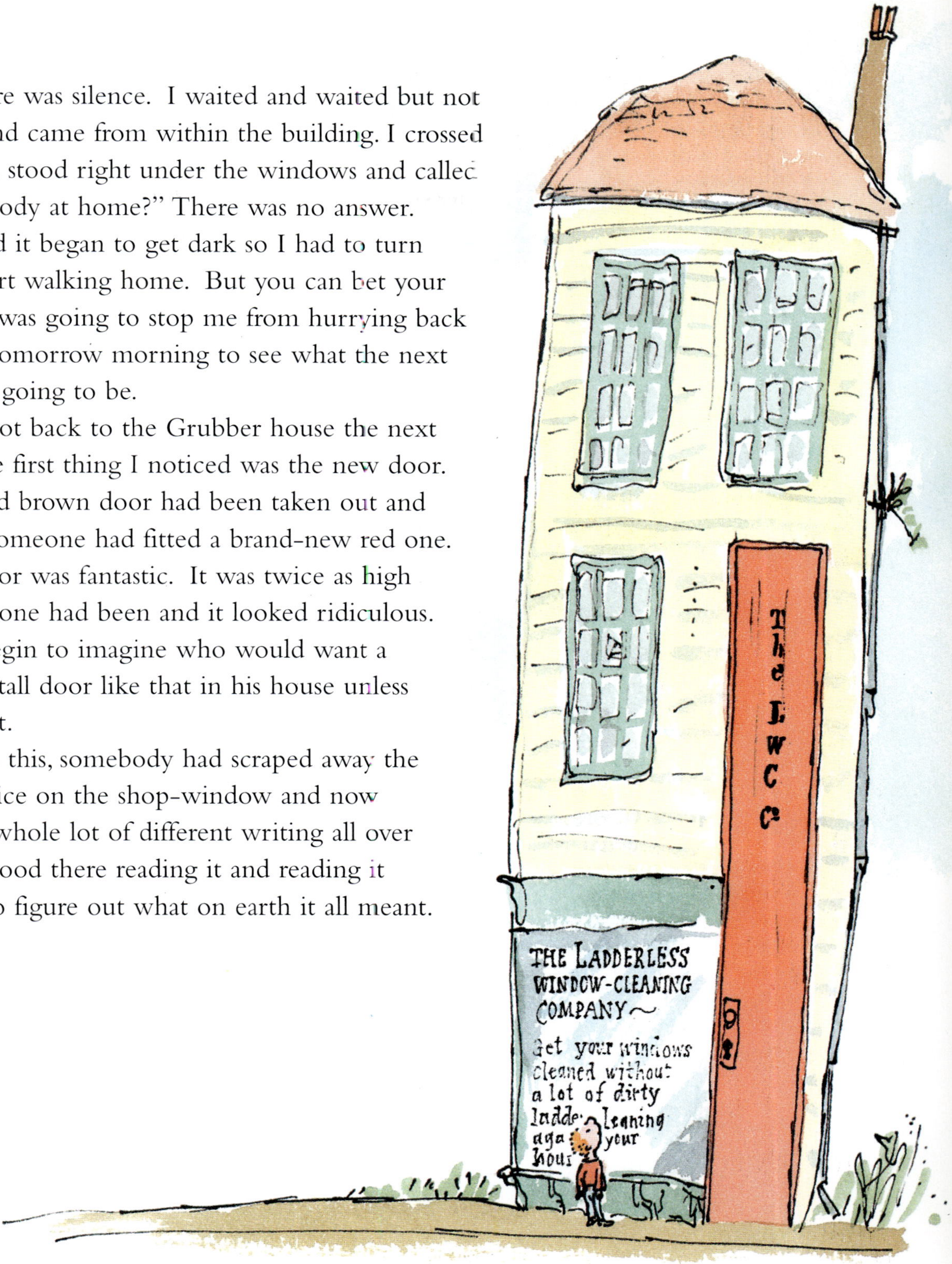

I tried to catch some sign or sound of movement inside the house but there was none ... until all of a sudden ... out of the corner of my eye ... I noticed that one of the windows on the top floor was slowly beginning to open outwards ...

Then a HEAD appeared at the open window.

I stared at the head. The head stared back at me with big round dark eyes.

Suddenly, a second window was flung wide open and of all the crazy things a gigantic white bird hopped out and perched on the window-sill. I knew what this one was because of its amazing beak which was shaped like a huge orange-coloured basin. The Pelican looked down at me and sang out:

"Oh how I wish
For a big fat fish!
I'm as hungry as ever could be!
A dish of fish is my only wish!
How far are we from the sea?"

"We are a long way from the sea," I called back to him, "but there is a fishmonger in the village not far away."

"A fish *what*?"

"A fish*monger*."

"Now what on earth would that be?" asked the Pelican. "I have heard of a fish-*pie* and a fish-*cake* and a fish-*finger*, but I have never heard of a fish-*monger*. Are these mongers good to eat."

This question baffled me a bit, so I said, "Who is your friend in the next window?"

"She is the Giraffe!" the Pelican answered. "Is she not wonderful? Her legs are on the ground floor and her head is looking out of the top window!"

As if all this wasn't enough, the window on the *first floor* was now flung wide open and out popped a Monkey!

The Monkey stood on the window-sill and did a jiggly little dance. He was so skinny he seemed to be made only out of furry bits of wire, but he danced wonderfully well, and I clapped and cheered and did a little dance myself in return.

"We are the Window-Cleaners!" sang out the Monkey.

"We will polish your glass
Till it's shining like brass
And it sparkles like sun on the sea!
We are quick and polite,
We will come day or night,
The Giraffe and the Pelly and me!

We're a fabulous crew,
We know just what to do,
And we never stop work to drink tea.
And your windows will glow
When we give them a go,
The Giraffe and the Pelly and me!

We use water and soap
Plus some kindness and hope,
But we never use ladders, not we.
Who needs ladders at all
When you're thirty feet tall?
Not Giraffe, and not Pelly! Not me!"

I stood there enthralled. Then I heard the Giraffe saying to the Pelican in the next window, "Pelly, my dear, be so good as to fly down and bring that small person up here to talk to us."

At once the Pelican spread his huge white wings and flew down on to the road beside me. "Hop in," he said, opening his enormous beak.

I stared at the great orange beak and backed away.

"GO ON!" the Monkey shouted from up in his window. "The Pelly isn't going to *swallow* you! Climb IN!"

I said to the Pelican, "I'll only get in if you promise not to shut your beak once I'm inside."

"You have nothing to fear!" cried the Pelican,

"And let me tell you why.
I have a very special beak!
A special beak have I!
You'll never see a beak so fine,
I don't care where you go.
There's magic in this beak of mine!
Hop in and don't say NO!"

"I will *not* hop in," I said, "unless you swear on your honour you won't shut it once I'm inside. I don't like small dark places."

"When I have done what I am just about to do," said the Pelican, "I won't be *able* to shut it. You don't seem to understand how my beak works."

"Show me," I said.

"Watch this!" cried the Pelican.

I watched in amazement as the top half of the Pelican's beak began to slide smoothly backwards into his head until the whole thing was almost out of sight.

"It bends and goes down inside the back of my neck!" cried the Pelican. "Is that not sensible? Is it not magical?"

"It's unbelievable," I said. It's exactly like one of those metal tape-measures my father's got at home. When it's out, it's straight. When you slide it back in, it bends and disappears."

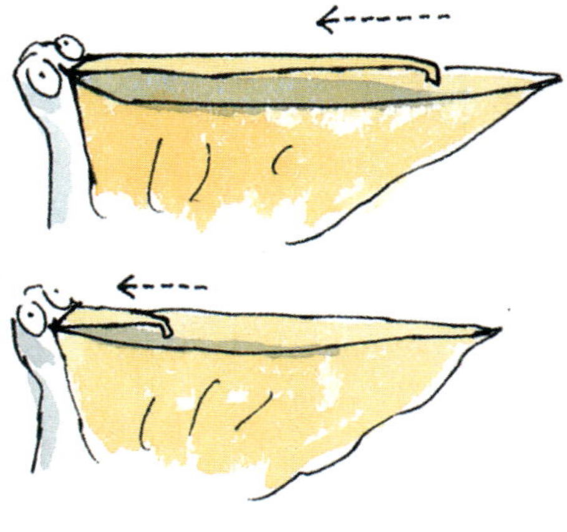

"Precisely," said the Pelican. "You see, the top half is of no use to me unless I am chewing fish. The bottom half is what counts, my lad! The bottom half of this glorious beak of mine is the bucket in which we carry our window-cleaning water! So if I didn't slide the top half away I'd be standing around all day long holding it open!

"So I slide it away
For the rest of the day!
Even so, I'm still able to speak!
And wherever I've flown
It has always been known
As the Pelican's Patented Beak!

If I want to eat fish
(That's my favourite dish)
All I do is I give it a tweak!
In the blink of an eye
Out it pops! And they cry,
'It's the Pelican's Patented Beak!"

"Stop showing off down there!" shouted the Monkey from the upstairs window. "Hurry up and bring that small person up to us! The Giraffe is waiting!"

I climbed into the big orange beak, and with a swoosh of wings the Pelican carried me back to his perch on the window-sill.

The Giraffe looked out of her window at me and said, "How do you do? What is your name?"

"Billy," I told her.

"Well, Billy," she said, "we need your help and we need it fast. We *must have* some windows to clean. We've spent every penny we had on buying this house and we've got to earn some more money quickly. The Pelly is starving, the Monkey is famished and I am perishing with hunger. The Pelly needs fish. The Monkey needs nuts and I am even more difficult to feed. I am a Geraneous Giraffe and a Geraneous Giraffe cannot eat anything except the pink and purple flowers of the tinkle-tinkle tree. But those, as I am sure you know, are hard to find and expensive to buy."

The Pelican cried out, "Right now I am so hungry I could eat a stale sardine!

"Has anyone seen a stale sardine
Or a bucket of rotten cod?
I'd eat the lot upon the spot,
I'm such a hungry bod!"

Every time the Pelican spoke, the beak I was standing in jiggled madly up and down, and the more excited he got, the more it jiggled.

The Monkey said, "What Pelly's *really* crazy about is salmon!"

"Yes, yes!" cried the Pelican. "Salmon! Oh, glorious salmon! I dream about it all day long but I never get any!"

"And *I* dream about walnuts!" shouted the Monkey. "A walnut fresh from the tree is so scrumptious-galumptious, so flavory-savory, so sweet to eat that it makes me all wobbly just thinking about it!"

At exactly that moment, a huge white Rolls-Royce pulled up right below us, and a chauffeur in a blue and gold uniform got out. He was carrying an envelope in one gloved hand.

"Good heavens!" I whispered. "That's the Duke of Hampshire's car!"

"Who's he?" asked the Giraffe.

"He's the richest man in England!" I said.

The chauffeur knocked on the door of The Grubber.

"We're up here!" the Giraffe called down to him.

He looked up and saw us. He saw the Giraffe, the Pelly, the Monkey and me all staring down at him from above, but not a muscle moved in his face, not an eyebrow was raised. The chauffeurs of very rich men are never surprised by anything they see. The chauffeur said, "His Grace the Duke of Hampshire has instructed me to deliver this envelope to The Ladderless Window-Cleaning Company."

"That's us!" cried the Monkey.

The Giraffe said, "Be so good as to open the envelope and read us the letter."

The chauffeur unfolded the letter and began to read, "'Dear Sirs, I saw your notice as I drove by this morning. I have been looking for a decent window-cleaner for the last fifty years but I have not found one yet. My house has six hundred and seventy-seven windows in it (not counting the greenhouses) and all of them are filthy. Kindly come and see me as soon as possible. Yours truly, Hampshire.' That," added the chauffeur in a voice filled with awe and respect, "was written by His Grace The Duke of Hampshire in his own hand."

The Giraffe said to the chauffeur, "Please tell His Grace The Duke that we will be with him as soon as possible."

The chauffeur touched his cap and got back into the Rolls-Royce.

"Whoopee!" shouted the Monkey.

"Fantastic!' cried the Pelican. "That must be the best window-cleaning job in the world!"

"Billy," said the Giraffe, "what is the house called and how do we get there?"

"It is called Hampshire House," I said. "It's just over the hill. I'll show you the way."

"We're off!" cried the Monkey. "We're off to see the Duke!"

The Giraffe stooped low and went out through the tall door. The Monkey jumped off the window-sill on to the Giraffe's back. The Pelican, with me in his beak hanging on for dear life, flew across and perched on the very top of the Giraffe's head. And away we went.

It wasn't long before we came to the gates of Hampshire House, and as the Giraffe moved slowly up the great wide driveway, we all began to feel just a little bit nervous.

"What's he like, this Duke?" the Giraffe asked me.

"I don't know," I said. "But he's very very famous and very rich. People say he has twenty-five gardeners just to look after his flower-beds."

Soon the huge house itself came into view, and what a house it was! It was like a palace! It was bigger than a palace!

"Just look at those windows!" cried the Monkey. "They'll keep us going for ever!"

Then suddenly we heard a man's voice a short distance away to the right. "I want those big black ones at the top of the tree!" the man was shouting. "Get me those great big black ones!"

We peered round the bushes and saw an oldish man with an immense white moustache standing under a tall cherry tree and pointing his walking-stick in the air. There was a ladder against the tree and another man, who was probably a gardener, was up the ladder.

"Get me those great big black juicy ones right at the very top!" the old man was shouting.
"I can't reach them, Your Grace," the gardener called back. "The ladder isn't long enough!"
"Damnation!" shouted the Duke. "I *was* so looking forward to eating those big ones!"

"Here we go!" the Pelican whispered to me, and with a swish and a swoop he carried me up to the very top of the cherry tree and there he perched. "Pick them, Billy!" he whispered. "Pick them quickly and put them in my beak!"

The gardener got such a shock he fell off the ladder. Down below us, the Duke was shouting, "My gun! Get me my gun! Some damnable monster of a bird is stealing my best cherries! Be off with you, sir! Go away! Those are *my* cherries, not yours! I'll have you shot for this, sir! Where *is* my gun?"

"Hurry, Billy!" whispered the Pelican. "Hurry, hurry, hurry!"

"My gun!" the Duke was shouting to the gardener. "Get me my gun, you idiot! I'll have that thieving bird for breakfast, you see if I don't."

"I've picked them all," I whispered to the Pelican.

At once the Pelly flew down and landed right beside the the furious figure of the Duke of Hampshire, who was prancing about and waving his stick in the air!

"Your cherries, Your Grace!" I said as I leaned over the edge of the Pelican's beak and offered a handful to the Duke.

The Duke was staggered. He reeled back and his eyes popped nearly out of their sockets. "Great Scott!" he gasped. "Good Lord! What's this? Who are *you*?"

And now the Giraffe, with the Monkey dancing about on her back, emerged suddenly from the bushes. The Duke stared at them. He looked as though he was about to have a fit.

"*Who are these creatures?*" he bellowed. "Has the whole world gone completely dotty?"

"We are the window-cleaners!" sang out the Monkey.

"We will polish your glass
Till it's shining like brass
And it sparkles like sun on the sea!
We will work for Your Grace
Till we're blue in the face,
The Giraffe and the Pelly and me!"

"You *asked* us to come and see you," the Giraffe said.

The truth was at last beginning to dawn on the Duke. He put a cherry into his mouth and chewed it slowly. Then he spat out the stone. "I like the way you picked the cherries for me," he said. "Could you also pick my apples in the autumn?"

"We could! We could! Of course we could!" we all shouted.

"And who are *you*?" the Duke said, pointing his stick at me.

"He is our Business Manager," the Giraffe said. "His name is Billy. We go nowhere without him."

"Very well, very well," the Duke muttered. "Come along with me and let's see if you're any good at cleaning windows."

I climbed out of the Pelican's beak and the kindly old Duke took me by the hand as we all walked towards the house. When we got there, the Duke said, "What happens next?"

"It is all very simple, Your Grace," the Giraffe replied. "I am the ladder, the Pelly is the bucket and the Monkey is the cleaner. Watch us go!"

With that, the famous window-cleaning gang sprang into action. The Monkey jumped down from the Giraffe's back and turned on the garden tap. The Pelican held his great beak under the tap until it was full of water. Then, with a wonderful springy leap the Monkey leaped up once again on to the Giraffe's back. From there he scrambled, as easily as if he were climbing a tree, up the long long neck of the Giraffe until he stood balancing on the very top of her head. The Pelican remained standing on the ground beside us, looking up at the Giraffe.

"We'll do the top floor first!" the Giraffe shouted down. "Bring the water up, please."

The Duke called out, "Don't worry about the two top floors. You can't reach them anyway."

"Who says we can't reach them?" the Giraffe called back.

"I do," the Duke said firmly, "and I'm not having any of you risking your silly necks around here."

If you wish to be friends with a Giraffe, never say anything bad about its neck. Its neck is its proudest possession.

"What's wrong with my neck?" snapped the Giraffe.

"Don't argue with me, you foolish creature!" cried the Duke. "If you can't reach it, you can't reach it and that's the end of it! Now get on with your work!"

"Your Grace," the Giraffe said, giving the Duke a small superior smile, "there are no windows in the world I cannot reach with this magical neck of mine."

The Monkey, who was dancing about most dangerously on top of the Giraffe's head, cried out, "Show him, Giraffey! Go on and show him what you can do with your magical neck!"

The next moment, the Giraffe's neck, which heaven knows was long enough already, began to grow longer . . .

and LONGER . . .

and LONGER . . .

and LONGER . . .

and HIGHER . . .

and HIGHER . . .

and HIGHER . . .

until at last the Giraffe's head with the Monkey on top of it was level with the windows of the top floor.

The Giraffe looked down from her great height and said to the Duke, "How's that?"

The Duke was speechless. So was I. It was the most magical thing I had ever seen, more magical even than the Pelican's Patented Beak.

Up above us, the Giraffe was beginning to sing a little song, but she sang so softly I could hardly catch the words. I think it went something like this:

"My neck can stretch terribly high,
Much higher than eagles can fly.
If I ventured to show
Just how high it would go
You'd lose sight of my head in the sky!"

The Pelican, with his huge beak full of water, flew up and perched on one of the top-floor window-sills near the Monkey, and now the great window-cleaning business really began.

The speed with which the team worked was astonishing. As soon as one window was done, the Giraffe moved the Monkey over to the next one and the Pelican followed. When all fourth-floor windows on that side of the house were finished, the Giraffe simply drew in her magical neck until the Monkey was level with the third-floor windows and off they went again.

"Amazing!" cried the Duke. "Astonishing! Remarkable! Incredible! I haven't seen out of any of my windows for forty years! Now I shall be able to sit indoors and enjoy the view!"

Suddenly I saw all three of the Window-Cleaners stop dead in their tracks. They seemed to freeze against the wall of the house. None of them moved.

"What's happened to them?" the Duke asked me. "What's gone wrong?"

"I don't know," I answered.

Then the Giraffe, with the Monkey on her head, tiptoed very gingerly away from the house and came towards us.

The Pelican flew with them. The Giraffe came up very close to the Duke and whispered, "Your Grace, there is a man in one of the bedrooms on the third floor. He is opening all the drawers and taking things out. He's got a pistol!"

The Duke jumped about a foot in the air. "Which room?" he snapped. "Show me at once!"

"It's the one on the third floor where the window is wide open," the Giraffe whispered.

"By Gad!" cried the Duke. "That's the Duchess's bedroom! He's after her jewels! Call the police! Summon the army! Bring up the cannon! Charge with the Light Brigade!" But even as he spoke the Pelican was flying up into the air. As he flew, he turned himself upside down and tipped the window-cleaning water out of his beak. Then I saw the top half of that marvellous patented beak sliding out of his head, ready for action.

"What's that crazy bird up to?" cried the Duke.

"Wait and see," shouted the Monkey. "Hold your breath, old man! Hold your nose! Hold your horses and watch the Pelly go!"

Like a bullet the Pelican flew in through the open window, and five seconds later out he came again with his great orange beak firmly closed. He landed on the lawn beside the Duke.

A tremendous banging noise was coming from inside the Pelican's beak. It sounded as though someone was using a sledgehammer against it from the inside.

"He's got him!" cried the Monkey. "Pelly's got the burglar in his beak!"

"Well done, sir!" shouted the Duke, hopping about with excitement. Suddenly he pulled the handle of his walking-stick upwards, and out of the hollow inside of the stick itself he drew a long thin sharp shining sword. "I'll run him through!" he shouted, flourishing the sword like a fencer. "Open up, Pelican! Let me get at him! I'll run the bounder through before he knows what's happened to him! I'll spike him like a pat of butter! I'll feed his gizzards to my foxhounds!"

But the Pelican did not open his beak. He kept it firmly closed and shook his head at the Duke.

The Giraffe shouted, "The burglar is armed with a pistol, Your Grace! If Pelly lets him out now he'll shoot us all!"

"He can be armed with a *machine-gun* for all I care!" bellowed the Duke, his massive moustaches bristling like brushwood. "I'll handle the blighter! Open up, sir! Open up!"

Suddenly there was an ear-splitting BANG and the Pelican leaped twenty feet into the air. So did the Duke.

"Watch out!" the Duke shouted, taking ten rapid paces backwards. "He's trying to shoot his way out!" And pointing his sword at the Pelican, he bellowed, "Keep that beak closed, sir! Don't you dare let him out! He'll murder us all!"

"Shake him up, Pelly!" cried the Giraffe. "Rattle his bones! Teach him not to do it again!"

The Pelican shook his head so fast from side to side that the beak became a blur and the man inside must have felt he was being scrambled like eggs.

"Well done, Pelly!" cried the Giraffe. "You're doing a great job! Keep on shaking him so he doesn't fire that pistol again!"

At this point, a lady with an enormous chest and flaming orange hair came flying out of the house screaming, "My jewels! Somebody's stolen my jewels! My diamond tiara! My diamond necklace! My diamond bracelets! My diamond earrings! My diamond rings! They've had the lot! My rooms have been ransacked!" And then this massive female, who fifty-five years ago had been a world-famous opera-singer, suddenly burst into song.

"My diamonds are over the ocean,
My diamonds are over the sea,
My diamonds were pinched from my bedroom,
Oh, bring back my diamonds to me."

We were so bowled over by the power of the lady's lungs that all of us, excepting the Pelican, who had to keep his beak closed, joined in the chorus.

"Bring back, bring back,
Oh, bring back my diamonds to me, to me.
Bring back, bring back,
Oh, bring back my diamonds to me!"

"Calm yourself, Henrietta," said the Duke. He pointed to the Pelican and said, "This clever bird, this brilliant burglar-catching creature saved the day! The bounder's in his beak!"

The Duchess stared at the Pelican. The Pelican stared back at the Duchess and gave her a wink.

"If he's in there," cried the Duchess, "why don't you let him out! Then you can run him through with that famous sword of yours! I want my diamonds! Open your beak, bird!"

"No, no!" shouted the Duke. "He's got a pistol! He'll murder us all!"

Someone must have called the police because suddenly no less than four squad cars came racing towards us with their sirens screaming.

Within seconds we were surrounded by six policemen, and the Duke was shouting to them, "The villain you are after is inside the beak of that bird! Stand by to collar him!" And to the Pelican he said, "Get ready to open up! Are you ready . . . steady . . . *go*! Open her up!"

The Pelican opened his gigantic beak and immediately the policemen pounced upon the burglar who was crouching inside. They snatched his pistol away from him and dragged him out and put handcuffs on his wrists.

"Great Scott!" shouted the Chief of Police. "It's the Cobra himself!"

"The who? The what?" everyone asked. "Who's the Cobra?"

"The Cobra is the cleverest and most dangerous cat-burglar in the world!" said the Chief of Police. "He must have climbed up the drainpipe. The Cobra can climb up anything!"

"My diamonds!" screamed the Duchess. "I want my diamonds! Where are my diamonds?"

"Here they are!" cried the Chief of Police, fishing great handfuls of jewellery from the burglar's pockets.

The Duchess was so overcome with relief that she fell to the ground in a faint.

When the police had taken away the fearsome burglar known as the Cobra, and the fainting Duchess had been carried into the house by her servants, the old Duke stood on the lawn with the Giraffe, the Pelican, the Monkey and me.

"Look!" cried the Monkey. "That rotten burglar's bullet has made a hole in poor Pelly's beak!"

"That's done it," said the Pelican. "Now it won't be any use for holding water when we clean the windows."

"Don't you worry about that, my dear Pelly," said the Duke, patting him on the beak. "My chauffeur will soon put a patch over it the same way he mends the tyres on the Rolls. Right now we have far more important things to talk about than a little hole in a beak."

We stood there waiting to see what the Duke was going to say next.

"Now listen to me, all of you," he said. "Those diamonds were worth millions! Millions and millions! And *you* have saved them!"

The Monkey nodded. The Giraffe smiled. The Pelican blushed.

"No reward is too great for you," the Duke went on. "I am therefore going to make you an offer which I hope will give you pleasure. I hereby invite the Giraffe and the Pelican and the Monkey to live on the estate for the rest of their lives.

"I shall give you my best and largest hay-barn as your private house. Central heating, showers, a kitchen and anything else you desire for your comfort will be installed.

"In return, you will keep my windows clean, and pick my cherries and my apples. If the Pelican is willing, perhaps he will also give me a ride in his beak now and again."

"A pleasure, Your Grace!" cried the Pelican. "Would you like a ride now?"

"Later," said the Duke. "I'll have one after tea."

At this point, the Giraffe gave a nervous little cough and looked up at the sky.

"Is there a problem?" asked the Duke. "If there is, do please let me hear it."

"I don't like to sound ungrateful or pushy," murmured the Giraffe, "but we do have one very pressing problem. We are all absolutely famished. We haven't eaten for days."

"My *dear* Giraffey!" cried the Duke. "How very thoughtless of me. Food is no problem around here."

"I'm afraid it's not quite as easy as all that," said the Giraffe. "You see I myself happen to be . . ."

"Don't tell me!" cried the Duke. "I know it already! I am an expert on the animals of Africa. The moment I saw you I knew you were no ordinary giraffe. You are of the Geraneous variety, are you not?"

"You are absolutely right, Your Grace," said the Giraffe. "But the trouble with us is that we only eat . . ."

"You don't have to tell me that either!" cried the Duke. "I know perfectly well a Geraneous Giraffe can eat only one kind of food. Am I not right in thinking that the pink and purple flowers of the tinkle-tinkle tree are your only diet?"

"Yes," sighed the Giraffe, "and that's been my problem ever since I arrived on these shores."

"That is no problem at all here at Hampshire House," said the Duke. "Look over there, my dear Giraffey, and you will see the only plantation of tinkle-tinkle trees in the entire country!"

The Giraffe looked. She gave a gasp of astonishment, and at first she was so overwhelmed she couldn't even speak. Great tears of joy began running down her cheeks.

"Help yourself," said the Duke. "Eat all you want."

"Oh, my sainted souls!" gasped the Giraffe. "Oh, my naked neck! I cannot *believe* what I am seeing!"

The next moment she was galloping full speed across the lawns and whinnying with excitement and the last we saw of her, she was burying her head in the beautiful pink and purple flowers that blossomed on the tops of the trees all around her.

"As for the Monkey," the Duke went on, "I think he also will be pleased with what I have to offer. All over my estate there are thousands of giant nut trees . . ."

"Nuts?" cried the Monkey. "What kind of nuts?"

"Walnuts, of course," said the Duke.

"***Walnuts!***" screamed the Monkey. "Not *walnuts*? You don't really mean *walnuts*? You're pulling my leg! You're joking! You can't be serious! I must have heard wrong!"

"There's a walnut tree right over there," the Duke said, pointing.

The Monkey took off like an arrow, and a few seconds later he was high up in the branches of the walnut tree, cracking the nuts and guzzling what was inside.

"That leaves only the Pelly," said the Duke.

"Yes," said the Pelican nervously, "but I'm afraid that what I eat does not grow on trees. I only eat fish. Would it be too much trouble, I wonder, If I were to ask you for a reasonably fresh piece of haddock or cod every day?"

"Haddock or cod!" shouted the Duke, spitting out the words as though they made a bad taste in his mouth. "Cast your eyes, my dear Pelly, over there to the south."

The Pelican looked across the vast rolling estate and in the distance he saw a great river.

"That is the River Hamp!" cried the Duke. "The finest salmon river in the whole of Europe!"

"***Salmon!***" screeched the Pelican. "Not *salmon*? You don't really mean *salmon*?"

"It's *full* of salmon," the Duke said, "and I own it. You can help yourself."

Before he had finished speaking the Pelican was in the air. The Duke and I watched him as he flew full speed towards the river. We saw him circle over the water, then he dived and disappeared. A few moments later, he was in the air again, and he had a gigantic salmon in his beak.

I stood alone with the Duke on the lawn beside his great house. "Well, Billy," he said, "I'm glad they are all happy. But what about you, my lad? I am wondering if you happen to have just one extra special little wish all for yourself. If you do, I'd love you to tell me about it."

There was a sudden tingling in my toes. It felt as though something tremendous might be going to happen to me any moment.

"Yes," I murmured nervously. "I do have one extra special little wish."

"And what might that be?" said the Duke in a kindly voice.

"There is an old wooden house near where I live," I said. "It's called The Grubber and long ago it used to be a sweet-shop. I have wished and wished that one day somebody might come along and make it into a marvellous new sweet-shop all over again."

"Somebody?" cried the Duke. "What do you mean, *somebody*? You and I will do that! We'll do it together! We'll make it into the most wonderful sweet-shop in the world! And *you*, my boy, will own it!"

Whenever the old Duke got excited, his enormous moustaches started to bristle and jump about. Right now they were jumping up and down so much it looked as though he had a squirrel on his face. "By Gad, sir!" he cried, waving his stick, "I shall buy the place today! Then we'll all get to work and have the whole thing ready in no time! You just wait and see what sort of a sweet-shop we are going to make out of this Grubber place of yours!"

It was amazing how quickly things began to happen after that. There was no problem about buying the house because it was owned by the Giraffe and the Pelly and the Monkey, and they insisted upon giving it to the Duke for nothing.

Then builders and carpenters moved in and rebuilt the whole of the inside so that once again it had three floors. On all these floors they put together rows and rows of tall shelves, and there were ladders to climb up to the highest shelves and baskets to carry what you bought.

Then the sweets and chocs and toffees and fudges and nougats began pouring in to fill the shelves. They came by aeroplane from every country in the world, the most wild and wondrous things you could ever imagine.

There were Gumtwizzlers and Fizzwinkles from China, Frothblowers and Spitsizzlers from Africa, Tummyticklers and Gobwangles from the Fiji Islands and Liplickers and Plushnuggets from the Land of the Midnight Sun.

For two whole weeks the flood of boxes and sacks continued to arrive. I could no longer keep track of all the countries they came from, but you can bet your life that as I unpacked each new batch I sampled it carefully. I can remember especially the Giant Wangdoodles from Australia, every one with a huge ripe red strawberry hidden inside its crispy chocolate crust ... and the Electric Fizzcocklers that made every hair on your head stand straight up on end as soon as you popped one into your mouth ... and there were Nishnobblers and Gumglotters and Blue Bubblers and Sherbet Slurpers and Tongue Rakers, and as well as all this, there was a whole lot of splendid stuff from the great Wonka factory itself, for example the famous Willy Wonka Rainbow Drops – suck them and you can spit in seven different colours. And his Stickjaw for talkative parents. And his Mint Jujubes that will give the boy next door green teeth for a month.

On the Grand Opening Day, I decided to allow all my customers to help themselves for free, and the place was so crowded with children you could hardly move. The television cameras and the newspaper reporters were all there, and the old Duke himself stood outside in the road with my friends the Giraffe and the Pelly and the Monkey watching the marvellous scene. I came out of the shop to join them for a few moments and I brought each of them a bag of extra-special sweets as a present.

To the Duke, because the weather was a little chilly, I gave some scarlet Scorchdroppers that had been sent to me from Iceland. The label said that they were guaranteed to make the person who sucked them as warm as toast even if he were standing stark naked at the North Pole in mid-winter. The moment the Duke popped one into his mouth, thick smoke came gushing out of the old boy's nostrils in such quantities that I thought his moustaches were going up in flames. "Terrific!" he cried, hopping about. "Tremendous stuff! I'll take a case of them home with me!"

To the Giraffe I gave a bag of Glumptious Globgobblers. The Globgobbler is an especially delicious sweet that is made somewhere near Mecca, and the moment you bite into it, all the perfumed juices of Arabia go squirting down your gullet one after the other. "It's wonderful!" cried the Giraffe as a cascade of lovely liquid flavours poured all the way down her long long throat. "It's even better than my favourite pink and purple flowers!"

To the Pelican I gave a big bag of Pishlets. Pishlets, as you probably know, are bought by children who are unable to whistle a tune as they walk along the street but long to do so. They had a splendid effect upon the Pelican, for after he had put one of them into his beak and chewed it for a while, he suddenly started singing like a nightingale. This made him wildly excited because Pelicans are not song-birds. No Pelican had ever been known to whistle a tune before.

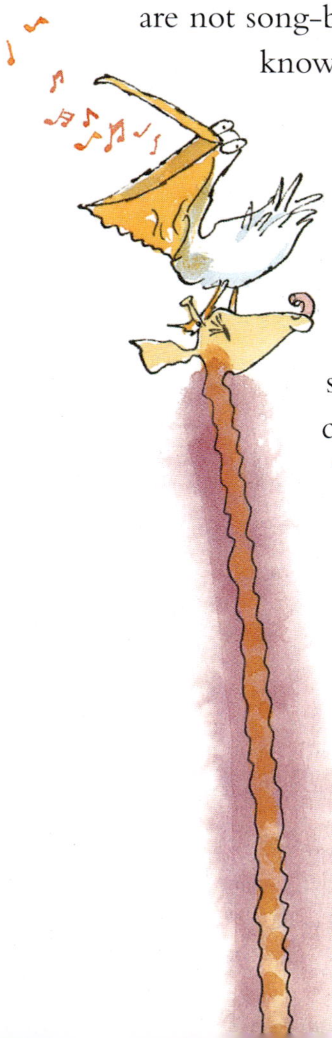

To the Monkey I gave a bag of Devil's Drenchers, those small fiery black sweets that one is not allowed to sell to children under four years old. When you have sucked a Devil's Drencher for a minute or so, you can set your breath alight and blow a huge column of fire twenty feet into the air. The Duke put a match to the Monkey's breath and shouted, "Blow, Monkey, blow!" A sheet of orange flame shot up as high as the roof of the Grubber house and it was wonderful.

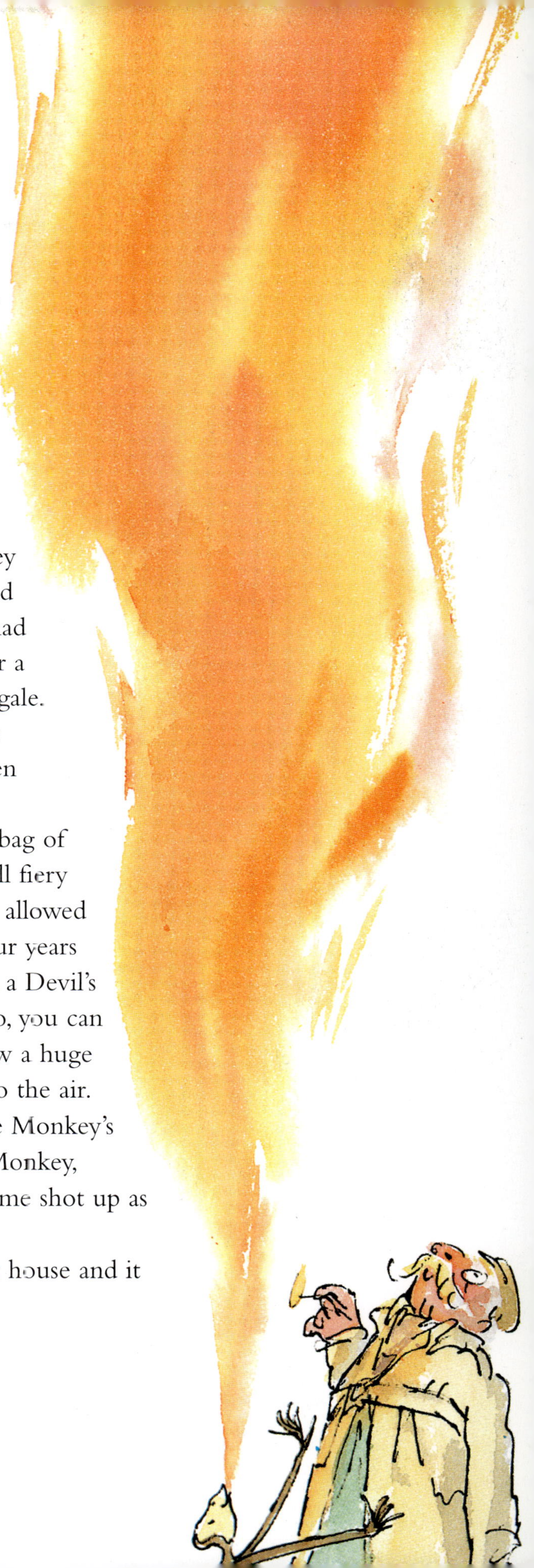

"I've got to leave you now," I said. "I must go and look after my customers in the shop."

"We must go, too," said the Giraffe. "We have one hundred windows to clean before dark."

I said goodbye to the Duke, and then one by one I said goodbye to the three best friends I had ever had. Suddenly, we all became very quiet and melancholy, and the Monkey looked as though he was about to cry as he sang me a little song of farewell:

"We have tears in our eyes
As we wave our goodbyes,
We so loved being with you, we three.
So do please now and then
Come and see us again,
The Giraffe and the Pelly and me.

All you do is to look
At a page in this book
Because that's where we always will be.
No book ever ends
When it's full of your friends
The Giraffe and the Pelly and me."

There's more to Roald Dahl than great stories . . .

Did you know that 10% of author royalties* from this book go to help the work of the Roald Dahl charities?

Roald Dahl's Marvellous Children's Charity exists to make life better for seriously ill children because it believes that every child has the right to a marvellous life.
This marvellous charity helps thousands of children each year living with serious conditions of the blood and the brain – causes important to Roald Dahl in his lifetime – whether by providing nurses, equipment or toys for today's children in the UK, or helping tomorrow's children everywhere through pioneering research.
Can you do something marvellous to help others?

Find out how at **www.marvellouschildrenscharity.org**

The Roald Dahl Museum and Story Centre, based in Great Missenden just outside London, is in the Buckinghamshire village where Roald Dahl lived and wrote. At the heart of the Museum, created to inspire a love of reading and writing, is his unique archive of letters and manuscripts. As well as two fun-packed biographical galleries, the Museum boasts an interactive Story Centre. It is a place for the family, teachers and their pupils to explore the exciting world of creativity and literacy.

Find out more at **www.roalddahlmuseum.org**

The Roald Dahl's Marvellous Children's Charity (RDMCC) is a registered charity no. 1137409.
The Roald Dahl Museum and Story Centre (RDMSC) is a registered charity no. 1085853.
The Roald Dahl Charitable Trust, a newly established charity, supports the work of RDMCC and RDMSC.

*Donated royalties are net of commission